Irresistible

Woman

II

By

J. W. Smith

ISBN-13: 978-0692200094
ISBN-10: 0692200096

Dedication

I would like to first thank God for giving me the will power to complete this novel. I'd like to personally thank the writers who came before me and paved the road for a determined man to travel on.

Secondly, I would like to send a special thank you to my three children, Tyquan Cashe', Jernisha Lashune and Jherica Sharell Smith
for loving their father, unconditionally.
Also, my first grandbaby, Serenity Olivia Smith.
'Love you. Serenity!

I'd like to thank the lovely Lakeisha Mitchell for putting up with my hectic workload while I was getting this book completed.

I'd also like to thank the editor, Ernestine Rose for bringing her professionalism to this novel.

Finally, I'd like to give a SHOUT-OUT
To the avid readers that support great reads!

NO LOVE LOST and *IRRESISTIBLE WOMAN I*
was the start of a never ending career in the literary world!
THANK YOU, READER

Preface

The ***Irresistible Woman*** series is about family. There are families we are born with, and families that are made by circumstance. We all have irresistible women in our families, those that charm us and entertain us, and who capture our undying devotion. Some families even have irresistible men.

But we also have relatives that we wish we didn't know. They come around when we don't want to see them, demanding money, or favors, or both. Sometimes they hurt us, or they hurt themselves, forcing us to rescue them once again. They act out at family gatherings, usually drunk or high, and embarrass us. And while we'd really like to disown them (and sometimes do), they are still family.

Real family is not determined by blood. That's an accident of birth.
Real family is made up of the people who nurture us, who give of their time, and their energy, and their love. They are there for us without asking; they are loyal to a fault. There are in-laws and blended families, foster families and adopted families. There are "play" cousins, and "play" sisters and brothers. There are "homies" that grew up in the neighborhood, and lifelong friends with the common bond of team, gang, army, or prison. Families come in all shapes and sizes, birthed from a variety of reasons.

Welcome to the family, a crazy collection of characters, devotion, dysfunction, and all.

J.W.Smith

Irresistible Woman II

Chapter 1

It was an unusually stormy afternoon in July of 2002 when a beautiful three-pound, six-ounce Devianna Chakira Barnes was born to Ms. Cynthia K. Powell-Barnes. With the biological father listed as deceased on the birth certificate, Cynthia declared herself a widow and attached the Barnes family name to the back of hers. She contemplated her future as a young mother left behind to bear the burden of carrying the financial stability alone. Perplexed as to why she hadn't spoken with Devon's only living heir since the funeral, her emotions allowed the feeling of abandonment to seep into her consciousness, completely rendering her venerable. On a promise to enjoy the "fruits of life," the words of Paulette, her middle-school friend, on Aug 14, 2002, Cynthia boarded a Grey Hound bus to the city of imminent danger; unknowingly approaching the pitfalls of top notch game. The two and a half day bus ride to California didn't help, either. Her mind was slowly deteriorating as the large bus pulled into the terminal and the driver announced the time, date and location before exiting to assist the passengers waiting to board. Cynthia wrapped the baby in her blanket and stood to get off when the dingily-dressed youngster sitting at the back of the bus approached her.

"You need some help, Little Mama?"

"No, I'm fine, thanks." She quickly responded and hurried to exit the bus, not wanting to be the last one.

"Is that my girl?" The young woman hollered across the parking lot as Cynthia exited the bus with a tiny Devianna snuggled against her breast.

"Paulette James, is that you?" Cynthia responded with sheer excitement in her voice. "It's me, girl, and I'm all woman." Paulette twirled completely around like a contestant in a beauty pageant.

"You haven't aged a day. You look wonderful!"

"How's my dear friend doing?"

"I suppose I'm doing alright under the circumstances," Cynthia responded with obvious signs of confusion.

"It's all good girlfriend. What doesn't kill you only makes you strong enough to deal with the rest of the bullshit we are destined to encounter along the way. Let me see that precious baby!"

Paulette pulled the soft pink blanket from Devianna's face and there she was, a beautiful brown-eyed baby girl. She was rocking a pink and white paisley dress, pink socks with the ruffles on top and a princess crown that neatly adorned the full head of tiny curls. Baby Devianna began to cry at the first sight of Paulette's face as if she knew the woman had a hidden agenda.

"Aw, Auntie didn't mean to wake that baby. Look at those beautiful brown eyes. She's gorgeous!"

The wells of Cynthia's eyes began to mist, thinking of what Devon left behind. "Thank you so much. She's all the memory I have left of that man."

"Look, spilled milk is just what it is. Gone. Goodbye. You have to start thinking of the good life and leave the past in the past. Come on. We're parked right over here. I'll ask Boss to get your suitcases." Paulette was playing hard ball and her take-charge attitude was in full effect.

"Who might this Boss be, if may I ask?"

"He's a good friend of mine and a business-minded person, I must say."

The two stroll the full length of the bus and Cynthia stopped, gazing out into the parking lot to see what Paulette was rolling in.

"Are you in that beautiful ride?"

"Yeah, girl. That's one of Boss's many toys. I told him I was going to the bus station to pick up a good friend of mine from back home and his crazy ass insisted on bringing me up here. He said he wants all my friends to start off experiencing the good life the moment they step on the California soil. Boss is a special kind of guy, but one thing I can say about him, he's definitely a man that handles his business."

Paulette reached the fully loaded 2002 Range Rover squattin' on the 26 inch Gottis and opened the door.

"Daddy, will you be so kind to get her suitcases from under the bus?"

"I can certainly assist the beautiful young lady with that request." Boss replied. He hopped out of the Rover and stared into the back window at his newest prospect, anticipating fucking her into submission.

Boss was a twenty-five-year-old child prodigy from the Bay Area with a suave appeal to every menacing thing he did. The witty young man left most six feet under. He graduated part of the class of '98 from the prestigious NYU with a double major in psychology and biology. Boss was a health-nut with the physique of a Greek god. His IQ was once rated a point and half above Albert Einstein's when he was in junior high school. Boss was very precocious and by the tender age of six months, he taught himself to walk. When he was in his first year of middle school, he'd finish his lessons within ten minutes of each class, threatening the mama's boys for the rest of the period. Boss was given the government name Lester Bellefonte III at the time of birth, but quickly adapted to the moniker "Boss" for his take-charge attitude as a growing boy. Boss could out-think most of his peers on a bad day.

He returned to the truck with the luggage in tow and loaded the bags into the trunk of the Rover.

"Thank you so much, Mr. Boss," Cynthia said, totally naive to the fact that people used slang names most of the time to protect their true identity.

"I have your best interest in mind, Star. You can just lay back, kick it, and enjoy the ride," the young man continued with a menacing grin plastered on his mug. Boss was absolutely smitten to see his bottom bitch had laced the newbie up with the house rules, and from the sound of her melodic tone, she was down with the program. Boss studied women closely. He could recognize when a broad was in dire need of a father figure. He was sharp enough to become their "way in" when they were looking for a way out.

Boss traveled the forty-five-minute drive to the first street on the long winding road of upscale homes. Cynthia's eyes lit up like a Christmas tree at the sight of the beautiful houses. Unable to contain herself from the sheer excitement of seeing the elegantly manicured lawns of Hollywood Hills, Cynthia dove in head first.

"Paulette, is this where you live?"

"Yeah, girl, you didn't know? I told you the California lifestyle is off the chain and I meant that. Boss bought this home about a year ago. The girls and I have had a blast so far putting our ideas together and getting the designer to come in to make it happen. Now that you've come to town, I'm sure Boss won't mind for you to add your professional touch. I know you know fashion'"

"Say no more! This beautiful lady can have whatever her heart desires." Boss looked back at Cynthia and nodded his approval.

"Thank you so much, Paulette, for rescuing me! And Mr. Boss, you are such an amazing man for inviting me to your home."

Boss reclined his seat back, resting his chin on one hand and extending the other on the steering wheel. He nodded to "Happy Feelings" by Frankie Beverly and Maze.

Cynthia sat in the back of the Rover, elated to know that her longtime friend and close confidant of the last few weeks was there to help her pick up the shattered pieces of her life. Feeling like Paulette was the only non-judging ear, Cynthia had revealed some of her darkest secrets, allowing herself to be vulnerable and easily susceptible to dangerous game. After the birth of her precious daughter, the two decided the best thing for the distraught mom to clear her hard feelings was to cut ties with any and everyone associated with her deceased husband. Paulette assured Cynthia that she had her back to the fullest, reiterating that the California lifestyle was off the chain and getting money would not be a problem.

Boss pulled into the winding driveway of his ten-bedroom mansion with the six-car garage. Cynthia gasped at the breathtaking site. Boss peeped into his rearview mirror and realized that the house alone solidified her willingness to become a part of his organization. Cynthia covered the baby's head and scooted out the back seat. She stood in the driveway of the home for several minutes admiring its massiveness. Being a country girl from Texas, she had only seen this kind of home on MTV Cribs' most pricey pads. Boss, always a gentleman, grabbed her suitcases from the opened trunk.

"Wow! This is an amazing home! Mr. Boss, you must be the C.E.O. of a Fortune 500 company to live like this!"

"I do a little something to keep the bills paid around here." Boss replied. As a true player in the game, he would always downplay his role to the fullest, all the way up until the moment his prey awakened and then his attitude turned from sugar to shit.

Cynthia was escorted in and introduced to the other eight residents of The Chocolate Swirl. She looked around in amazement at the high ceilings and beautiful chandeliers that dangled from them. She was momentarily suspended on cloud nine, amazed at the confidence that each of the ladies standing before her exuded. She drifted off momentarily, faintly recalling digging through her father's collection of movies and watching the "The Mack" where Goldie required all of his high-profile prostitutes to live in a mansion. Without dwelling on it, she dismissed the theory, figuring the bald-faced youngster couldn't have been a day older than twenty-five.

Boss walked over to the intercom and ordered the bartender to bring a round of ten for him and the girls to celebrate. He was finally ten deep in his stable of thoroughbreds, loving every minute of it. The drinks were served and Boss raised his glass in the air.

"I toast to financial freedom." He lowered the glass to his side and the ladies automatically dismissed themselves to resume their responsibilities. Boss, Paulette and an unsuspecting Cynthia relaxed in the spacious living area, chatting while they finished their drinks. Boss told his soon-to-be victim that she was welcome to stay as long as she needed to get back on her feet. Little did she know that he meant that literally?

"I want you to know that there is no rush or time limit, that should make you feel as if you've overstayed your welcome, and there's no pressure for you to have to spend anything other than your precious time getting yourself together. *Mi casa es su casa*."

"Again, I truly appreciate you for inviting me into your home.

I really needed this change in direction," Cynthia replied.

"It's all good. No, I must thank you for coming into my world, sweet lady." Boss winked at Cynthia and strolled off towards his massive master suite.

Months went by and the ladies were entertaining clients around the clock, all hours of the night. Cynthia was given the fabulous Queen's Suite situated on the southern wing of the mansion. The young mother was allowed free reign of the home which made her feel as though she was living a Hollywood fantasy. Monday through Friday, she was up by six A.M. to breastfeed baby Devianna and to prepare her day. On the weekend, Boss afforded her unlimited shopping resources during their supervised trips to the mall. It was his courtesy card to all newbies that entered his world as a permanent resident.

One evening, with a storm brewing on the outside, Paulette entered the Queen's Suite with two glasses in her hand. A bottle of wine was tucked under her right arm.

"Hey, girl! How's that baby?" Paulette asked.

"She's fine. She does get a little irritated from all the movement in the hall late at night. What's going on in this house?" Cynthia asks.

"Here. Have a glass of wine and relax your nerves before you get on mines!" Paulette blurted out.

"Thank you. I really need this, being stressed out and all."

Cynthia turned and laid the infant down on the bed. She turned back and cupped the glass with both hands. The two engaged in conversation about their childhood experiences for a few minutes when the effects of crushed Molly hit Cynthia like a ton of bricks. She began to sweat profusely and every word that escaped her mouth was a slur. She tried to get to her feet, but quickly realized that she was unable to stand on her own. She fell back on the bed, head circling like a whirlwind. She looked up at Paulette who was now hovering over her, seemingly amused at her inability to control herself. Determined to escape the feeling of not having control of her circumstances, against her better judgment, she again tried to get to her feet. This time, she lumbered face first onto the plush carpet. Having done this on several occasions,

Paulette knew she had fifteen minutes before Cynthia would regain consciousness. She stepped over the unconscious woman and spoke into the intercom.

"Your order of one bitch out cold is prepared and ready to be served, Daddy."

Within minutes, Boss walked in and instructed his bottom bitch to take the baby to the maid's quarters. Paulette quickly obliged and exited the room with the crying infant cradled in her arms.

Boss lifted his prey off the carpet by her arms, dragged her over to the bed, and tossed her limp body on top. He ripped her clothes off and entered her, fucking her immobile body like there was no tomorrow. Cynthia finally came to, as she felt a sharp pain of Boss's dick pounding her abdomen with force. She was terrified to see the young man on top of her going to town.

"What the hell are you doing? Get the fuck off me, mother fucka!" Cynthia screamed, swinging both hands wildly.

"Calm down, bitch! Your ass is Daddy's girl, now!"

Cynthia tried to shift her hips to get away from Boss's penis and angered the womanizer into a fit of rage. He back-handed her in the mouth and immediately drew blood. But Cynthia wasn't the average girl to go down without a fight. She mustered up the brute force of a linebacker and pushed the muscular man off her. She rolled off the bed and crawled to her feet, but the horned menace was right on her heels. He reached out and grabbed her around the neck, but Cynthia slipped from the grip of his headlock and swung a hay-maker to his face, missing his dome by inches. Again she met the carpet face first. Boss straddled her back and dropped a hammer fist to the cranium, causing Cynthia pace to be slowed. Once she had shaken the daze, Cynthia elbowed her attacker in the mouth and scrambled back to her feet, determined to get away by any means necessary. She sprinted to the door, snatched it open, and made it into the hallway where she was met with the 1000-volt stun gun Paulette twirled in her hand.

"Where you call yourself going, Missy?" Those were the last words Cynthia heard before hitting the floor.

Boss exited the room and palmed Paulette's ass with both

hands. Exhausted from the scuffle, he rested on her shoulder and commended his bottom bitch for being on point. Boss, angry from the feeling of disrespect dragged Cynthia's naked body back into the room.

"Put the bitch on a bread and water diet for a few weeks. By then her attitude should be as soft as one of you hoe's ass." He spat out through clinched teeth.

Chapter 2

Samantha and the others boarded a flight home. They were returning from a festive weekend in Florida. Unlike their stay while on the run, Trevon enjoyed himself to the fullest. On their flight back, he sat gazing out of the small framed window confused as to where Cynthia had up and run off to. He was disgusted with himself for not going to check on her after she'd birthed his brother's seed, but the loss of his other half, kept him in deep depression and most times living close to the edge.

After returning home and getting a few things taken care of, Trevon put out a hefty reward throughout the hood for any information leading to Cynthia and the baby's whereabouts. Within hours, he started to receive calls of possible sightings, but each time it was nothing more than a false lead or a ploy to mischievously inherit the reward money. Trevon sat in the media room swarmed with guilt for not being there for his niece and her mother. With mounting stress on his shoulders, he opened the laptop, logged in as Jonetta showered, and prepared to leave. Once Jonetta was dressed she made her rounds to her husband's favorite spot in the home. She eased up the stairs, careful not to make a sound. She reached the top of the stairs and entered the media room startling Trevon. She proceeded forward and Trevon abruptly slammed the laptop closed, pulling his shirt down to hide himself. To her dismay she caught him masturbating to a porn site on the laptop. Jonetta took a mental note of his actions. The fact that he shut the computer down so abruptly, was what worried her even more, but the witty woman chose not to mention what she had seen.

"I'm going over to Sam's for a few hours. Would you like me to pick you up something to eat while I'm out?" Jonetta asked, staring down at the bulge under her husband's shirt.

"Naw, I'm cool." Trevon stuttered as he noticed Jonetta watching him.

"Ok. Well, I'll see you later." Jonetta turned and made her way back down the stairs, grabbing her keys and exiting out through the garage.

Thirty-five minutes later, she sat outside her sister's crib. She hit the speed dial on her phone for "Bad Bitch," and the phone rang.

"Hey, girl! Are you out there?"

"Yeah. Hit the garage." Jonetta responded.

Sam opened the garage and Jonetta pulled in beside the Benz.

"Hey, Sis," Sam said as she stood inside the garage door.

"What do you have to eat in there?"

"I didn't know you were hungry. I would've fixed you up some of my super love potion with a pile of spaghetti strewn on top to savor the flavor. My bad, had I known, I would've had you ready to get yo' grub on when you hit the door." Samantha continued on, shocked at the look on her sister's face.

"I'm your sister chick, not a potential lover. You should've put that super love potion on Marcus, Thomas Black, and Big Twin and uh uh ......"

"Ok, already! What kind of inspirational talk is that for a bitch that's been down with you since the mud pies days?"

"You know Mama Dee would've said the same thing."
Utter silence fell over the room as both Jonetta and Samantha drifted off in their own fond memories of Mama Dee's antics.

"I miss Mama." Samantha said.

"That's what I used to tell your crazy ass all the time that you were going to miss her when she's gone. Now look at you. You see exactly what I mean."

"I just wish I could've told her I was sorry for the shit I caused her to have to go through before she left here."

Just then, Samantha's phone rang. She looked down at the number but didn't recognize the 310 area code, so she put it back on the counter.

"I thought it may have been Clef. He called early this morning talking crazy."

"What's his problem?"

"They finally set his bond at a million and a half."

"What the hell did they charge him with?"

"Two counts of malicious murder in the act of committing a crime. He's got one for Lil Jonathan and one for Mama."

"He's not the person that fired the actual shots that killed either one of them, is he? The police were correct?"

"Yeah, but Leon said Texas law states ' in the commission of a crime, any living willing participants are to be held culpable for the outcome regardless of who fired the shot.'"

"What kind of time is he facing?"

"None, if I can help it." Samantha responded with a sinister look smeared across her face.

Chapter 3

Cynthia awoke to find herself sprawled out on the plush carpet ass-naked. The right side of her face was in excruciating pain and her vagina dripped an off-white creamy substance. She sat up on her elbows to focus on the spinning room, still partially dazed from the impact of the high power voltage. She scanned the large area looking for her baby, but there was no sight of Devianna anywhere. Realizing the baby was missing, panic started to set in. She scooted across the carpet to the edge of the bed, grabbing the comforter to pull herself up. She cried out for help, but there were no sign of rescue. She sat up thinking for the rest of the evening, contemplating on how to get her daughter back and fight her way out of this living nightmare. Later in the night, she forced herself out the bed and crawled into the restroom to clean her wounds. She entered the bathroom, grabbed the top of the sink to lift her up and was shocked at the sight of the cuts and bruises on her face. Cynthia cried out, begging for her grandmother's God to intervene in the mayhem she was going through. Balling into a fetal position, she cried herself to sleep.

Early the next morning, the door opened and a metal plate with two slices of bread and a warm cup of water was slid into the room. Cynthia exited the bathroom at the sound of the open door and stared at the metal plate in disbelief. She beat on the closed door for several minutes, but there was complete silence on the other end. As she headed back to the bed, the intercom came on.

"Calm down, bitch, and get your mind right!"

"Where's my baby?" The angry woman yelled out at the top of her lungs.

"The baby's fine. You're the one tripping. Lie down and get yourself some rest. You got some catching up to do when you get your mind right."

"Is my baby ok?" Cynthia screamed into the intercom. But there was no response. She cried out the entire morning until she was physically drained, depriving herself of the ability to challenge

Boss's authority.

In the following days, Cynthia was forced to eat stale bread and drink tap water for breakfast, lunch and dinner to survive. This caused her mind to further deteriorate. Once the reality set in, she became a basket case at best. She could not believe her childhood friend had set her up like this.

A few days later, clad in his white Hugh Hefner signature robe, Boss entered the Queen's Quarters, looking for some action. Cynthia cringed, but her body was much too weak to fight off his advances. He straddled her frail physique and fucked her until he felt his release coming. Then he slipped out of her vagina and shoved his dick down her throat, momentarily disabling her flow of breath. Seeing the woman helplessly struggle for oxygen, Boss jerked his dick out of Cynthia's mouth and with a menacing grin on his face, he whispered in her ear.

"Bitch is you ok? Do you need some mouth to mouth?"

Cynthia was in a dysfunctional state. Her mind was racing a mile a minute, wondering what the hell she'd gotten herself into. She blamed Devon and her mother for leaving her behind, and her brother-in-law for not being there, to shield her from this menace. She couldn't have ever imagined in her wildest dreams that her life would become so unbearable.

Days later, Boss entered the room a total different person. The better side of his bipolar disorder was in full swing. His words were charming and mysteriously inviting.

"Baby, is everything good?"

Yes," Cynthia muttered." I'm good."

She was floored by the audacity of this punk having the nerve to ask her such a question, knowing damn well she wasn't alright. Hell, she was being forced to perform sex acts against her will!

She was being raped! Her brain registered the words "Hell, no!" but her mental state was unable to endure any more of his wrath. Having lost twelve pounds during her latest punishment phase, Cynthia's had slipped in and out of consciousness, making her easily susceptible to manipulation.

Once Boss received confirmation of the young woman's willingness to abide by his rules, he got on the intercom and ordered the maid to bring a full course meal to the Queen's Quarter. For the first few days, Cynthia was unable to eat without regurgitating. Paulette was force to feed her by hand. Whatever bond once existed between the two was now broken permanently. Cynthia had never known hatred like this. Her body shivered like a recovering heroin addict from the physical damages Boss has inflicted upon her.

On the third day of her recovery, Cynthia looked up at Paulette and with a tear lodged in her right eye. She began to speak through a strained voice.

"What are we doing here?"

"Look. What the fuck you complaining about? I told you the lifestyle was off the chain, so I figured you would've known to put your hustle boots on."

"Paulette, I don't know anything about hustling. My life before now was totally centered on Devon, prior to the baby."

"Cynthia, we're older now and it's about getting what's yours by any means necessary out here in this wicked world."

"'By any means necessary' shouldn't have to include destroying the woman in you to satisfy a man, that don't give a damn about you."

"Lighten up. It's not all that bad. When I first came to town, I was angry and disgusted just like you, but after the many beatings, I finally came to terms with myself and started believing I needed that security in a man."

"But Paulette, It's not the line of work I want to be in or have my daughter around."

"Bitch, listen here! Quit your bawling and get with the program! It is what it is!"

"It is what it is with you, but not with me. I'm going to get my daughter out of this hell hole one way or another, even if it costs me my life."

"You'll be leaving here in a body bag if it's up to Boss. Here! Eat the rest of your dinner," Paulette grumbled as she shoved the remainder of the croissant roll into Cynthia's mouth.

After thirty days, seven hours and twenty-three minutes of seclusion, Cynthia was upgraded to phase two of the house ladder. She was permitted to see the baby for an hour a day Monday through Friday and two hours a day on the weekend, pending the evaluation of her progress. Cynthia made it to phase three swallowing three to five ecstasy pills a day to coat the pain of being abused. Boss fucked her a couple of nights a week until he was confident that she was ready to start entertaining high-end clients. He was a man building accountability in his newest bitch.

Cynthia's first of many clients was an older Caucasian gentleman and a regular at the mansion. The two sat together in the front living area, closely monitored by the eye on the wall. Once their meal was prepared, Cynthia beckoned the john to join her at the round table and the two walked off hand-in-hand towards the lounge. A short distance into their stroll, Cynthia shook loose from her date, did a U-turn, and planted her back against the wall to avoid the cameras. With the pressure mounting, she nervously ran to the front door and jiggled the lock, but found that the mansion was virtually escape-proof. She revised her plan and quickly rejoined her date that was still standing in the hallway. Confused about the sudden movement, the john stared in disbelief, startled at her odd behavior. Cynthia resurfaced into the camera's view, swinging her arms as if everything was just fine. She hoped for her life that Boss hadn't seen her failed escaped attempt.

The couple finished their meal and entered the Queens Quarters for some dessert. The john unfastened the fifty-two inch

Italian belt, dropped his pants to his knees, and began to massage his penis. The sight alone gave Cynthia the quivers. She wanted to throw up the meal she'd just eaten. Feeling totally disrespected by the perverted gentleman, she excused herself to the bathroom to locate the bottle of pills to relax her nerves. She quickly found the bottle and slammed three pills down her throat. She needed an out-of-body experience to deal with the pressure of being forced to prostitute. Cynthia turned the faucet on and cuffed enough water to swallow the pills. She sat down on the toilet until her nerves calmed. The young mother took a deep breath and mechanically re-entered the bedroom. The pervert strapped on his condom, crawled on top of Cynthia, and pushed his pinky sized penis inside her. He pumped a total of seven strokes before shaking as if he were having a convulsion.

"Ooooooh! You the best! Thank you, Baby." He rolled off her and stared up at the ceiling out of breath.

Cynthia sprang from the bed and sprinted into the bathroom clutching her stomach. She fell to the floor sobbing uncontrollably, angry at God for allowing one man to carry out such demonic acts. She snatched the face towel from the rack and desperately tried to wipe away the feeling of being a whore from between her legs. With the thought of being permitted to see her daughter once a day lingering deep in her consciousness, Cynthia straightened up and forced herself to go back for more of his sick fantasy.

By the time she made it to the fourth phase, Cynthia was allowed to make restricted calls back home to her grandmother's number only. Boss made sure her calls were always during the time she shared with the baby, so there was never a question of the child's whereabouts. The phone calls were closely monitored by Boss and he warned Cynthia of the consequences if she disobeyed his direct order. She understood well and played her role to the fullest. On one particular call, her grandmother had a lot to tell her about what was going on in her old stomping grounds.

"I was looking at the news this morning and seen where the police caught the young man responsible for killing Parnell Jenkins. He was supposedly hiding somewhere in Florida. Last week, he was brought back to Texas to stand trial for the murder. Oh, it's back on now. Lord have mercy…..they have four people handcuffed together. It looks like two men and two young ladies. The newscaster said"……Mrs. Gardner paused to hear the television.

He said "The young man is charged with seventeen counts, including malice murder. The others were charged with……looks like……. harboring a fugitive and illegal flight to avoid prosecution. I feel so bad for Margaret. She was a long-time member of Strangers Rest Baptist Church until her husband was killed and then she just disappeared from the congregation altogether. The Pastor sent a few deacons by the home she was living in, but they came back and reported that it was cleaned out and on the market for sale. This young man on the television sort of resembles that baby's father of yours."

"Granny, you don't know any of those people."

"Isn't that baby by the young man you sent the picture of with you and him hugged up in the booth at the mall?"

"Yes, that's him." Cynthia replied, knowing her granny's mind was still in great condition.

"What's the guy's name that they have in custody, Granny?"

"I didn't get a chance to catch the names of any of the suspects, but I'm sure it'll be top story at five o'clock. I'll keep you posted. Do you have a number I can call you at, instead of always having to wait on you to call me? I get lonely sometimes and just want to hear your voice.

"Okay, Granny. I love you and tell the rest of the family the baby and I are fine." Cynthia yelled through the phone to over-talk her granny's request. She knew there was no way that Boss would allow an incoming call into the mansion unless it was strictly business and lining his pockets.

"Alright, Baby. Granny loves you, too. Ya hear? You take good care of yourself and don't let it take so long for you to call me back."

"I won't, Granny. Bye."

"Bye, Baby."

The call was disconnected and Cynthia sat on the edge of her bed drowning in a sea of misery, until a deep voice came bellowing through the intercom, interrupting her thoughts.

Well done, Bitch. Now let's get back to work. You have clients waiting to be satisfied."

Cynthia swallowed her pride along with the last of her pills and went through the motions with her next few clients.

One evening, Boss got on the intercom and told Cynthia she'd been upgraded. "I been peeping your performance and the clients are raving about your skills. I adore the woman you've become over the last few months and with that being said, you will now start servicing double the amount of clients than you had been."

Cynthia stood with a stoic look on her face. She was furious at Boss, but she held her tongue and focused mentally on how to escape.

The first of her new clients was a middle-aged white man and high ranking official for the City of Los Angeles Police Department. After enjoying a romantic dinner and returning to the room, Cynthia dipped into the restroom and swallowed five of the Vicodin pills Mrs. Annie had given her to get her nerves right. She eased out of the bathroom and mechanically disrobed herself. She pulled the cover back to join the john, her stare boring a hole through his chest as he jerked on his Vienna-sized dick. Disgusted to no end, Cynthia snapped at the disappointing sight and went off on Boss's "black card" trick.

"If you don't get your pale ass out of my bed, you tiny dick mutha fucka, I am going to scream! Fuck this! I'm not going to sit back and be forced to perform these trifling ass acts anymore! Why don't you take your tiny ass dick home to your wife?" Cynthia screamed.

The pills had her feeling invincible enough to be able to withstand a good ass-whipping. The john was caught off guard, stunned that any of Boss's women would have the nerve to talk so disrespectfully. He'd been around long enough to have seen the Boss on one of his tirades, and knew he didn't play when it came to business. The john leaped to his feet and looked at Cynthia as she sashayed off towards the bathroom, providing her one last opportunity to take care of business. She slammed the door behind her, assuring the man that she was standing her ground.

He slid his trousers on and headed out the door, fastening the top three buttons on his shirt. The client paced the length of the hallway annoyed at the disrespect, and when he rounded the corner, he ran right into Boss. He was leaning against the wall drilling his bottom bitch for her performance. Seeing the look on the man's face, Boss immediately stopped what he was doing to check on his money,

"Is everything alright, Sir?"

"Let me out of this rinky-dink place you call a business. I thought this was a professional establishment where the ladies were willing participants. I didn't realize you were forcing these girls to be whores."

"What the hell are you talking about?"

"Well, the one you call your sweet little stallion turned out to be one rotten-ass apple. She seems disturbed or distressed about her duties. I will not be returning to this house until you make sure you have your business in proper order."

"Mr. Randle, I can't sit here and apologize for the bitch's actions or for whatever may have gone down in the room, but one thing I can assure you is things will be handled right away."

"Hmph!" Randle uttered as he quickly moved towards the door.

A few minutes passed and Boss entered the Queen's Quarters, slamming the door behind him. The look on his face was sheer terror to Cynthia. She immediately went into a frenzy of reasoning, but Boss was in no mood for small talk. He started beating Cynthia to a blood pulp, dragging her by her hair through the room. He kicked and stomped on the young woman until there was no movement at all left in her body and then he stormed out the room. Cynthia, badly bleeding, lay moaning on the carpet for an hour, drifting in and out of consciousness.

Two hours later, Boss strolled through the hallway monitoring his broads' work and spotted the maid dusting the pictures of him and his entourage of prostitutes, ass-naked, on the mantle.

"Say, listen here, old lady. Go down to the Queen's Quarters and check on the new bitch, Paulette claimed she heard noises coming from the room a couple of hours ago. She may have fallen and bumped her face up against the wall or some shit."

"Yes sir." Mrs. Annie responded. She shoots off towards the south wing of the mansion to do as she was instructed. She got to the door and twisted the knob, but the door was locked. She nervously reached for the set of master keys on her belt loop and fumbled through several of the keys before finding the right one. Mrs. Annie had been around since the beginning of time and she knew any time the door was locked from the outside, one of the girl's was being disciplined. When she opened the door, the scene before her was horrendous. Large splatters of blood adorned the wall as if she was looking at a crime scene. Cynthia was balled up in a fetal position with locks of hair pulled from her scalp. The maid hurried in and closed the door behind her. She hurried over and kneeled down, hovering over the badly beaten body. Cynthia whimpered as she looked up at the one person she felt wouldn't hurt her.

"Oh, my God! What has he done to you?" Immediately the older woman began to pray over Cynthia.

The injured woman slowly raised her head up and with tears lodged in her eyes; Cynthia smiled at the kind words. The maid went into the bathroom and grabbed several towels from the closet. She searched through the medicine cabinet, locating the plastic bottle of peroxide and hurried back to Cynthia's side to clean her wounds. A full hour passed before Mrs. Annie felt that the young woman would survive the malicious attack.

"I'll come by to check on you during my rounds in the morning. Get you some rest."

"I really appreciate what you're doing for me, Mrs. Annie. You're the only person that really cares about me around here. Will you check on my baby for me and bring me a few more of those pain pills?"

"I'll be on the lookout for her on my rounds and I'll bring the pills to you in the morning."

"Thank you so much."

The older woman exited the room and was immediately confronted by Boss.

"A mutha fuckin' hour? What the fuck you think this is, old lady? We ain't running any emergency room around here!"

"But she needed my help..."

"She needed to handle her mutha fuckin' business! That's what she needed to do instead of fucking with my money. Now get your old ass somewhere and mind your own business before I have you around here seeing clients for your stay!"

Mrs. Annie scampered off with her head down and her mind racing towards Revenge Avenue. She was hurt by his words, but not at all shocked that he would go to the extent of assuring that his threats were carried out. Since they'd moved out of Compton and relocated to the Hollywood Hills mansion, she lived in constant fear of his daily threats.

For the next few mornings while making her rounds, the maid would spend an additional ten to fifteen minutes inside Cynthia's room. Most days she entered the room, Cynthia was on her knees praying her heart out.

One evening Mrs. Annie entered the room and she didn't see the young woman curled up under the comforter or on her knees praying.

"Cynthia? Cynthia, are you in here?"

Cynthia came out of the bathroom standing proud with a vibrant smile adorning her face. She had taken enough of the atrocious beatings. She'd spent most of her healing time under the bed, crying out her prayers to the Lord and was ready to battle Boss with all she had left in her to save her daughter.

"I'm here, Mrs. Annie, strong as ever." Cynthia responded standing butt naked.

The maid quickly shut the bedroom door and grabbed her around the neck." Are you ok?" She repeated several times and pointed at the intercom.

"Besides the physical scars, I'm stronger than ever." Cynthia whispered in her ear.

Once again, the two embraced and the older woman tear'd up. Feeling the drips on her shoulder Cynthia took a step back and pleaded with the maid to help her get free.

"Listen. You have to find a way to get me and my daughter out of here before he kills me."

The older woman turned and immediately headed for the door with arms stretched out, pointing at the intercom.

Cynthia rushed over to stop her from leaving, but the maid shut the door and locked it behind her. She was devastated to find that the only person she felt had her back wanted no parts of her issues. She fell to the floor and began to question God.

"Lord? Where are you when I really need you? You said you wouldn't put any more burdens on me than I could bear, but Father, right now I'm about to break. I can't do this anymore, God. It's not right and I'm not strong enough to continue on with this madness. It's immoral and unethical and you're letting him get away with it. God, where are you?"

The intercom came on and Boss spoke into it." Bravo, Bitch! I'm right here! And you don't have to call out long distance when I'm right down the hallway."

"You're not God, you bastard!" Cynthia screamed into the intercom.

"I'm the closest you'll ever get to know of one. I see you're still a little agitated for some strange reason."

"Cause, you beat the hell out of me mutha fucka! That's why I'm upset!"

"Look, when you rolled up to this big pretty mutha fucker, didn't you understand there were bills and responsibilities that needed to be handled?"

"I didn't come here to be no damn whore!"

"Why such use of harsh words to describe how I make my money?

"Just let me and my baby out of here and I can hitchhike my way back to Texas, if I have to."

"You may as well forget you ever lived in Texas because California is where you will remain for the rest of your existence here on earth!"

The intercom was shut off and the rest of Cynthia's pleas fell on deaf ears. She lay flat on her back looking up at the stucco on the ceiling, mind racing as to how she would get her child and make it out alive.

Chapter 4

Jonetta stood staring a hole through her sister, wondering what the hell was on her mind. She knew from past experiences that Sam conjured up thoughts that weren't always a solid plan of action, but more of her own spontaneous reasoning of why she was all in, usually because of some blind devotion.

"So tell me this. How do you figure to get that done when gambling Deb tried that same shit with Alfred Don and Boogie, and she ended up getting herself killed in the midst of the breakout? Even the broad at the wheel of the getaway car received a life sentence, with no possibility of parole.

"One of two ways, either we get in Big Kenny's old house and get the money he left behind, or by any means necessary, we reach him from the courtroom."

"Sam, you have lost your rabid ass mind! Neither of those plans will ever work. Didn't you hear anything I just said?"

"Yeah, I heard you, but where there's a will there's a way! And I'm willing! You just need to lead the way, Jonetta Sharell Davis."

Jonetta immediately understood that their third grade pact was activated. Sam's loyalty was beyond accepting no for an answer. The fact that Sam would handle her business with or without her is what she feared the most.

"Clef will be freed again on bail or with the folks hot on his trail. I mean that," Sam said, confirming her sister's fears.

"Give me a week or so. Let me take a look at things and I'll tell you what I think after we visit Mama Dee's gravesite this weekend. I want to see what she thinks about all of this."

Jonetta grabbed the twenty thousand she came for, wrapped it up in a plastic grocery sack, and stuffed it down in her jeans. She hugged her sister's neck and exited out through the garage to head home.

The weekend arrived and Mama Dee's gravesite was packed

with folks from all over town. It was the Queen's birthday and everyone that knew her was out in full force. The celebration was still going on after three hours, when most of the neighborhood hustlers led by Trevon and Samantha migrated their way over to pay homage at Big Twin's plot. Jonetta and a few stragglers stayed behind. With most of the crowd gone Jonetta, consumed in her own memory of Mama Dee, strolled over and kneeled down by the head stone for a chat with her one time mentor.

"I really miss you, Mama Dee. I'm so sorry that my actions of loving a man more than myself caused me to be absent in the wake of your homecoming. Mama Dee, when I was locked up, I prayed to the Lord every day, asking Him to remove the ungodly ways of my heart. Now that urge seems to be revisiting me through a very dear friend of mine, your daughter. Mama Dee, Samantha's asking me to go against the grain, and I'm confused as to how to handle this situation. She knows I love her with all my heart and would do anything for her, but I promised the Lord that I'd chill and just be a good wife and mother if He would let us out of that last jam we were in. What am I supposed to do?" Jonetta sat listening for a response of some kind, but after a few minutes, she realized there would be none. She rested against the headstone thinking of a way to commit without being involved. For the first time in her life, Jonetta was dumbfounded and had nowhere to turn for answers. She wiped the tears from her face, kissed Mama Dee's headstone, and dropped the last batch of flowers over her mother before walking off to join the others. She reached Devon's grave as the crowd began to disperse.

"Hey, Baby. How you doin?"

"I'm okay. But as I stood over the grave, I felt like Twin was trying to tell me something."

"Like what?" Jonetta asked.

"For some reason, I feel like it had something to do with Cynthia and the baby. She's been heavy on my mind lately."

"Yeah. Mine, too." Jonetta replied as she sat on the grass next to her husband.

She was puzzled, but not shocked at the message. She squeezed his hand as she saw a tear roll down his face.

One evening while the couples dined out, they discussed a new plan to get the money rolling in. The two were interested in investing some of Trevon's royalties into a new business venture to create a residual income and they wanted to consult with a lawyer for his professional advice. The four were seated in a corner section of the restaurant with an open view of the patrons coming and going. Leon was ordering their fourth round of drinks when Trevon thought he saw the woman he'd been longing to find. He slid out of the booth and rushed over to get a closer look at the slender woman with cold black hair. He reached out with open arms, attempting to get a hug. Visibly shaken by what seemed like an inappropriate advance from a drunken man, the young woman took a step back and knocked his hands down.

"Cynthia! Is that you?"

"No, Sir! My name is not Cynthia. You must have the wrong person!"

"Ma'am, I'm so sorry. I thought you were my sister-in-law."

"Is that the best game you could come up with?"

"It's not about any game, little sister. I am happily married to that beautiful queen sitting right over there. But thanks any way. Again, I am very sorry for invading your privacy."

Trevon walked away from what turned out to be just another case of mistaken identity. He slid into the booth next to Jonetta. He sat with his left hand resting on his chin in deep thought, replaying his brother's whispers from the grave in his head.

"Is everything alright, Trevon?" Mr. Haley asked.

"Yeah, I'm cool. I just thought that I saw someone I knew."

"She looks like Cynthia to me." Sam said.

"That's who I thought it was." Trevon responded happy to find out he wasn't tripping.

"I didn't think it was her even though she looks like her. I heard Cynthia went out to California with Paulette."

"Paulette James?" Jonetta interrupted.

"Yes. Paulette James from back in the we need to get our creep on, days."

"Excuse my French, but she's been hoeing out of all three

holes since middle school." Sam added.

Trevon sat quiet, closely listening to Sam as she recalled the many acts of misconduct Paulette was alleged to have been caught up in. His brother's cry from the grave lurked deep in his subconscious. Something wasn't quite adding up. He knew Paulette was brought up as a wild child that abided by no rules, while Cynthia was raised by her grandparents in a zero tolerance home. How in the world could the two have hooked back up after so many years? He searched his mind trying to remember Cynthia's grandmother, the gray-haired woman with the brown station wagon.

"Sam, when you get to the hood, spread the word that I'm adding a thousand dollars to the reward for anyone with reliable information on how to find Mrs. Wanda Pearl Powell. I think that's her name."

"Hell, I'll play her for a thousand, Baby Boy." Sam responded facetiously.

"Come on, Sam. Get real! I'm trying to find Cynthia's grandmother."

"Okay, then, I'll find her for the thousand." Sam blurted out.

The lawyer dropped his head and shook it from side to side. He knew his high octane twenty-seven-year-old voice of the less fortunate would say whatever came to her mind, whether it was accurate or not. But he had mad love for her anyway.

The couples finished their dinner and drinks and said their goodbyes before leaving the restaurant. Jonetta nibbled on Trevon's ear as the two strolled hand-in- hand through the parking lot.

As Jonetta got into the passenger side of the BMW, she whispered, "Babe, don't you worry. We will find Cynthia and the baby."

"I know we will, but for some reason I feel like she's in danger, and maybe that's the message Devon was trying to relay."

"Truthfully, I was thinking the same thing, especially when Sam mentioned she was somehow tied in with Paulette and has gone out to California."

"That's exactly what put me on alert. Cynthia wasn't used to the streets. She could've gone out there and gotten taken fast."

"Yeah, well let's see what Sam comes up with and in the meantime, I'll contact a private investigator to see if they can locate her whereabouts."

"Sounds like a plan."

Trevon sat quiet the entire way home. He was thinking of a way to find his people, before it was too late.

Chapter 5

Weeks turned into months without a word on the missing woman's whereabouts. Trevon would wake up at night sweating and out of breath, clearly afraid of something in his dreams.

One early morning, Trevon woke to the sound of his cell phone vibrating on the nightstand. He turned to look at the screen to see who was calling so early. It was 5:30 in the morning. Trevon put on a southern accent and answered it.

"Hello?" Trevon said with a nasal twang in his voice.

"Can I speak with Mr. Barnes, please?" It was the private investigator calling to announce that he had a possible location on Cynthia.

"This is he." Trevon quickly responded in his regular voice.

"I got word from an inside source that the young woman is being held captive inside the Chocolate Swirl Mansion in the Hollywood Hills of California. I hadn't been able get a visual on her as of yet, but I know the source is good. The women residing in the home aren't allowed to associate with anyone other than their assigned clients. It's supposedly another Bunny Ranch-style whore house for the upper echelon."

"Where do we go from here?" Trevon inquired as he knit his brows together in concern.

"I've made an appointment to get inside to see the girls, but for some strange reason, the owner denied my access on several occasions."

"Well, of course. If he's hustling women for prostitution, he's not going to want anyone associated with law enforcement in his place of business. That's just common sense."

"No, I tried calling to make an appointment as a client, but the person in charge always denied me. I contacted authorities to see if maybe there was anything they could assist me with, but they have yet to return my call."

"So what's your next move?"

"I have one more trick up my sleeve. I'm going to work it from a different angle to see if he bites. I will let you know soon enough how it turns out."

"Great! Keep me posted. I desperately need to find Cynthia and the baby."

"I most certainly will."

Trevon released the line and immediately gave his wife an update.

"That was the private investigator saying he may have located Cynthia and the baby."

"What? That's wonderful! When is she coming home?" Jonetta asked with excitement flowing through her voice.

"He claims he hasn't seen her yet, but was informed that she is possibly being held against her will inside some place called The Chocolate Swirl."

"The Chocolate Swirl, what kind of shit is that?"

"He said it was another Bunny Ranch-style operation in the Hollywood hills."

Silence fell. Both of them were deep in thought.

"So what's his next move?"

"He's supposed to have one last trick up his sleeve to get inside and try to see her."

"Do you think he's telling the truth, Trey?

"I don't know. He should've made more progress by now as much as I've been paying him. I'm gonna' give him a few more days. "

"Yeah. Well, if that doesn't work, I may have something up my sleeve." Jonetta responded with a sassy sense of authority.

"Shit we gon' be like Bonnie and Clyde then,' cause if the private investigator says she's in there, I'm getting up in there one way or another, by choice or by force."

"Don't even trip! Wifey's got your mutha fuckin' back to the fullest."

Jonetta grabbed her cell phone off the night stand, leapt to her feet, and headed to the kitchen.

She hit the #2 button on her cell and "Bad Bitch" popped up.

"Damn, Sis! What the hell you want this early in the morning? You couldn't have woken up in the wrong bed. So what's your problem?"

"Good morning, Sis. I'm fine and you? I'm so happy to see you were looking to hear from me this morning with such a warm and fuzzy greeting."

"Cut the crap. What do you want?"

"We may have to make a move to the West Coast to check on Cynthia before we take care of that other business."

"I thought the private investigator was working on finding her."

"He called this morning with information on where she's supposed to be, but he hasn't seen her yet."

"What the hell does that mean? He hasn't seen her yet! What the fuck? Has she barricaded herself in the house for some strange reason?"

"I don't really know the full details of why he hadn't seen her and he's been hunting her for months now. Trevon said the man said she was being held hostage in some place called The Chocolate Swerve or something like that."

"Are you talking about The Chocolate Swirl in Cali?"

"Yeah, that's it. The Chocolate Swirl, what the hell you know about that?"

"It was on the news about a year ago. I think at first the police were investigating the house as a possible drug spot when the neighbors of Hollywood Hills began to complain about the number of people coming and leaving the residence at all times of the night. It was later determined that it was an upscale whore house, where most the clients were either businessmen, police, lawyers or politically connected in some way."

"No shit! What was the outcome?"

"They supposedly left the owner alone when it became known that his little black book contained some high profile names that had been visiting the joint on a regular basis. I didn't hear anything else about it after that, and like I said, it's been almost a year ago."

"Damn! That sounds like some real live Madam Heidi Fleiss bullshit!" Jonetta shouted.

"I don't know what you're talking about. Heidi was a bad

bitch getting plenty of loot."

"Come on, Sam! You act as if I don't know the game. It's the oldest profession in the business, and where there are tricks; there will always be treasure for a real bitch to get paid. I taught you that a long time ago. You weren't listening too well back then."

"Okay. So what time you coming through? We still need to hit these malls and handle that before these gift cards go bad."

"Hold your horses. I'll be over there before nine o'clock."

"Alright. You want me to have some of my love potion brewed and stewed for breakfast?" Sam asked and started to giggle, amused at her own comment.

"I told you who you should've given that pot luck to, girlfriend. Your ass wouldn't be laid up over there man-less right now. That's why you're able to answer the phone so damn fast, because ain't nobody coming through setting that ass ablaze." Jonetta joked. Sam looks around, then at her cell phone. She was trying to figure out how the hell her sister knew she was man-less at the time.

Later that evening, Trevon sat in the media room going over a demo of the latest artist signed to Devon Entertainment when Jonetta came home.

"Trevon!" Jonetta called out.

"Babe, I'm upstairs in the media room."

"Okay. I was just checking on you. I'm going to take a shower."

Jonetta headed to the master bedroom where a pleasant surprise awaited her. On his way home from the studio, Trevon made a quick stop at the florist. He purchased a pound and a half of red rose petals, two dozen white long-stem roses, and a box of Chocolate Truffles. When he first came home, he spread the rose petals throughout the garden tub and strategically placed the long stem roses in the shape of a heart on the bed. Jonetta opened the bedroom door and was very impressed with Trevon's show of affection. She disrobed herself, dropped a few cubes of sea salt in the tub, and slid neck-deep into the vibrating jets of the water.

"Trevon Barnes!" She yelled out.

Trevon eased around the corner like a stalker and stood holding the box of chocolates in his hand, sucking on his bottom lip. He smiled with lust in his eyes at the beautiful woman surrounded only by suds.

Jonetta was always satisfied with the numerous ways her husband found to show his love for her. She was fulfilled in every way: mentally, emotionally, and physically.

"Babe, I really appreciate the man that you've grown to be," she purred. "The roses are simply gorgeous!" she continued as she moved the suds aside to reveal one shapely leg. Trevon nodded his approval. "It took me a while to determine the true worth of the woman in you, but once I did realize it, I knew it was time to step up to the plate and show you how much you mean to me."

"I hope you don't feel like you feel like you have to prove something to me," Jonetta said.

"After a while, I saw with my own eyes that it wasn't about the money with you."

"Trevon, it has never been about material things with you. I saw potential in you that you may not have even been aware of back then, and I see now it really wasn't about the money with you, either," Jonetta responded as her eyes met those of the love of her life. The "come fuck me" look had gotten his attention.

Trevon moved closer and leaned over the tub until their tongues intertwined. Feeling the warmth of ecstasy, Jonetta rose up out the water, nipples hardened, and stepped out the tub to get up close and personal with her man. Soaking wet, she caressed the back of his neck with her left arm and unsnapped the button on his pants with her right. She slowly unzipped his pants, closely watching every notch of the zipper with anticipation as it was released. She reached inside and stroked the full length of his manhood, coming to a resting point at the middle of his abdomen. She dropped to her knees and pulled the nine-inch sword out of its peep hole. She stroked it several times before guiding it to her mouth. The horny wife teased the tip of his head with a circular motion, driving Trevon out of his mind.

He unbuttoned the damp Ralph Lauren shirt and tossed it near the laundry basket, showing that he and his man stayed ready for a sexual invite on a moment's notice. He watched as Jonetta, now in full stride, took the bulk of his penis into her mouth. She licked around his scrotum area until every spot was moistened. Trevon grabbed the side of Jonetta's face with both hands and pulled her to him.

"Okay, Babe. You are going to make me blast this rifle off at you." Trevon warned. He stepped out of his jeans and into the warmth of the hot tub. He beckoned for her to join him. She stepped in and lay back in the water so aroused she allowed the thrust of the jets to pulsate against her pearl tongue until she climaxed.

The couple caressed each other in the spacious tub for over an hour before deciding to get out. Jonetta washed and stepped out the tub with Trevon right on her bumper. She made it to her side of the sink and peeped into the mirror feeling his hot breath on her back. Trevon reached out and grabbed Jonetta by the shoulder, spinning her around. He picked her up by the waist and slid her naked ass onto the granite counter top. He leaned forward and suckled her protruding nipples with a motion of his own until heavy breaths of air escape from her mouth. He maneuvered his way between her legs, tasting every inch of her inner thighs along the way. With her back against the mirror, licking her lips and massaging her nipples, Trevon spread her legs in a V-shape and pressed the tip of his tongue against her vagina.

Upon impact, Jonetta purred like a lost kitten. She lifted both legs over his shoulder and held his head tightly as his long tongue slithered around the lining of her walls, resting on her clit. He suckled her clit until her body began to shake uncontrollably. Then he pulled her body to the edge of the sink, with the back of her head resting against the mirror. Trevon stood back and watched the length of his cock as he entered her love box. He started with a slow rotation to work the full length of his monster inside her. Once Jonetta had taken him in, her muscles contracted gripping him tightly to slow his forward motion. He looped his arms around her waist and pumped until she erupted a second time. With their juices running down his anaconda, Trevon slid out of Jonetta and stood watching his cock as it impulsively jumped with a premature white substance seeping from its head.

"Wait! Wait! Hold up a minute!" Trevon panted, almost out of breath. Jonetta slid off the sink and with no hands, she took his penis into her mouth and bobbed on it until she heard the usual growl Trevon made when he is ready to release. His body vibrated like a beeper as he burst in his wife's mouth with pleasure. Jonetta swallowed every bit of her husband's juices. As she walked towards the bed, she looked back at a frozen Trevon, standing with his heart rate pounding a beat and a half above normal. After what seemed like an eternity, he finally regained his bearings, wiped himself off, and walked into the bedroom looking for Jonetta.

"Babe, I don't want any more of that there. That shit there, have a nigga stuck like I smoked a blunt or something, and it has my heart pumping too hard."

"You say that all the time, Daddy, and don't ever mean it. You are starting to sound like a drunk on New Year's morning."

Jonetta was waiting in bed with nothing on. Trevon rolled in beside her, cupping her ass in his warm hands. She ran her hands along his chest until they fell asleep in each other's arms.

Early the next morning, Trevon woke up with a hard-on, Anaconda aimed straight towards the sky. He rolled Jonetta onto her side to position her right, slid out of the bed, and grabbed the tube of KY Jelly to lubricate himself. He hovered over the bed stroking his nine-inch monster, mesmerized at the roundness of his wife's ass peeking out from under the cover. He eased back in the bed, propped her right leg up with his knee, and guided his penis inside her. Jonetta squirmed as Trevon stroked until the full length of his dick was inside her. He gently pushed her in the back to position her head forward, slipped his right arm around her waist, and stroked her kitty until she was dripping wet.

After the first thirty minutes of lovemaking, Trevon unleashed the wild beast within. He flipped Jonetta onto her stomach and straddled her back camel-style. He slid the dick back inside her and with both hands positioned on her shoulder; he pulled her upwards, fucking her brains out. Jonetta screamed an octave higher and louder each time the beefcake powered against her stomach. She bit down on the pillow as Trevon stretched his legs out towards her face and pushed all of him inside her, leaving nothing but balls bumping against her pussy. The curve in his dick made it easy to hit every spot. Trevon jumped up and down inside her as if he were riding a horse in the Kentucky Derby. Jonetta's legs began to shake in spurts, signaling a waterfall was coming. When he was ready to cum, he wrapped both hands around her sensuous bottom and hugged her tight. He shot a load off and Jonetta screamed in ecstasy, rolling out of the bed, legs shaking and mind rambling.

After a few minutes, she tried desperately to speak but the sounds had no meaning. She finally caught up with her train of thought. "Damn, Daddy! Where did you learn to do that?"

"Same school you learned to do that what you do so well."

"Yeah, well there's no way in the world Mama Dee could've ever taught you no shit like that. You got to have a big dick to make a bitch shake like she in the Harlem fest."

"Oh! Are you talking about that camel style I put on your ass? I learned that on my own. Remember my pops wasn't ever around to teach me and Big Bro a damn thing," Trevon strolled off and looked over his shoulder cock-eyed at his wife. Other than the occasional debates the couple had, their relationship was at an all-time high.

Jonetta was caught off guard at the sound of the house phone ringing. She trotted into the front office and grabbed the phone expecting a telemarketer. "Hello," she answered out of breath.

"Damn! You two must be humping or something! Both of yawl's phones are off and you answered the house phone sounding like you fresh out of oxygen. Bitch, I don't know C.P.R. You need to take a ten-count and calm your mutha fucken breathing down before you pass the fuck out."

"Sam, stop the madness! I ran up to the office to grab the phone, if you just insist on knowing why I sounded out of breath," Jonetta responded, knowing damn well that was a lie. Her legs were still shaky.

"Girl, you are not going to believe this shit. Guess who Leon has been hired to represent?"

"I don't know. Who is it, Clef?"

"Naw. His case probably won't make it to trial for another two years."

"Okay. Well? I ain't got time for the guessing game."

"It's Mr. Thomas Donnell Jordan himself and party of thirteen."

"Shut your mouth. The Federal agent got jammed up?"

"Yes, Bitch! Thomas D. Jordan aka Ernie Black and party of thirteen are all in federal custody as we speak." Sam replied.

"No way! What the hell did his police ass do to get in a jam?"

"Girl, that's what I thought at first, but towards the end of our little fling, some real shady shit was going on with him. He was coming in the crib with clothes torn like he had been in some sort of a scuffle. I started to wonder was he having a fight every night for a reason, because I couldn't understand how anyone was getting away with fighting with a federal agent without being killed. Anyway, today it all came out in the wash. He's been charged with seventeen counts of bank robbery and six counts of aggravated brandishing of a weapon in the commission of a crime. Leon held a press conference last night and it should be the top story on the news today at noon. It was a ring of task force and undercover officers caught up in a sting. Some were bank robbers and the others were robbing drug lords under the pretense that they were on duty. The indictment has Thomas D. Jordan listed as the kingpin of the case. It says he was the one distributing the payout once the jobs were done."

"He was the mastermind?"

"Evidently he was. I heard Leon talking to one of his colleagues about the case last night, and then this morning he left early saying he had to go see a client's wife about some money."

"So that's where all that money was coming from you were telling me about."

"Hell yeah! I just wish I would've known then what I know now! I would have taken my chances running off with one of them duffle bags full of U.S. currency. I thought it had something to do with the job and it had a tracking device on it. Especially after he snapped 'cause I peeked in it one time. Shit, I could've gone over to the Caribbean and got me one of them Shaba Ranks looking mutha fuckas hollering twelve inches are more! Got me some long beaded braids sown in and been laying up getting fed grapes and dick all day for the rest of my life."

"You know you would've been a bad ass Caribbean duffle bag-carrying whore for real then."
The two laughed so hard they both started crying.

Chapter 6

Mrs. Annie began her clean up on the north end of the mansion. It was the center location for the King's Quarters. She tapped on Boss's door with the ring of keys, but there was no answer. She used the master key to let herself in. She tipped in and scanned the room for any sight of the young man. After a full search of the large area was made, the maid's heart rate once again returned to normal. Mrs. Annie knew Boss was very precocious for his age, she nervously contemplated going through with her mission, mortally terrified of the consequences she faced. She had been viciously warned long ago to never be caught attempting to let one of the girls free. After she snapped back to reality, she decided that in this particular case, because of the baby right was right. She moved into action, making her way over to the master-intercom box to locate the knob for the Queen's Suite. Quickly finding it, she looked back at the door before putting her mouth directly on the speaker.

"Get ready to move in five minutes."

Cynthia rose to her elbows at the sound of the maid's muffled voice coming through the intercom. She paused, thinking of how unconcerned the older woman seemed a few days earlier. Her eyes widened like golf balls as she wondered if this was some sort of sadistic game being played out by Boss to see if she'd bite. She quickly determined that if caught, a beating was worth the risk to save her daughter.

Cynthia hadn't worn any sort of clothing since her last sanction was handed down a few weeks earlier. She gathered enough strength to get up and wrap the sheet around her slender frame. With every step she took, the young mother's eyes welled up at the thought of reuniting with her child. She wondered how the older woman would be able to get her out of the maid's quarters without being spotted by the care-taker cameras or any of the girls in the process. Out of desperation, Cynthia was mentally prepared to make a run for freedom. She grabbed the first garment she put her hands on, draped it around herself, and stood at attention, ready to move.

After several intense minutes of searching through Boss's personal belongings, Mrs. Annie located what she was looking for and nervously exited the King's Suite. She cautiously pushed the cart through the hallway, praying she made it to Cynthia's room before crossing paths with Boss. Finally, she reached the door and fumbled through the set of keys until she heard the lock disengaging. The door eased open and Cynthia stood barefoot awaiting her instructions. The maid pulled the cart inside the room and shut the door behind her, shaking as if she had Parkinson's disease. She reached under the cart to retrieve the size six walking shoes for Cynthia to put on. Mrs. Annie knew from experience that Boss had never allowed any of his stable to wear anything other than attire fit for a whore. He didn't want any of his broads running off using tennis shoes he paid for as their method of escape. All clients were seen in high heels, short skirts, and in many cases, nothing at all.

"Here, put these on."

"Where's my baby?" Cynthia asked with a frightened look on her face.

"She's in the maids' quarters. We need to move fast. Boss will be making his rounds soon."
Cynthia put her hand over Mrs. Annie's mouth and pointed at the intercom box.

"I turned it completely off for this room. Hurry up. We have to get a move on. If he catches either of us, they'll never find our bodies," Mrs. Annie whispered to Cynthia.

"Are you going?"

"No. I can't go. My life is here, I'll be alright, though. You just come on."

"I couldn't stand it if something happened to you because of me.

"Look. I'll be okay. Just hurry up before he catches us and we're both in trouble."

Cynthia forced her feet into the too-tight shoes and ducked inside the cart as instructed. Mrs. Annie took a deep breath, opened the door, and maneuvered around the cart to check for any sign of Boss. The coast was clear and the hallway was empty. She paused for a few seconds, but decided there was no turning back.

She shut the door behind her and headed up the hallway to the maid's quarters, sliding the cart up against the door to keep Cynthia hidden. There, she spotted the caretaker nodding in the corner. She quickly wrapped the baby in a fresh blanket, opened the door, and placed her in Cynthia's arms. Devianna's eyes opened wide and she smiled. The nervous woman closed the door behind her, giving them more time to maneuver without being seen. She focused on the last task, and that was to get Cynthia and the baby to freedom. As she proceeded up the hallway, she made it past the first camera, and the alarm sounded. Mrs. Annie quickly dialed in the six-digit code and shut off the alarm. She left the cart parked behind the camera and stepped back into view alone, in case Boss was watching. Heart pounding, she made it to the second camera. There was no turning back now. At the back door, she fumbled through the keys until she found the right one. She opened the door and Cynthia slid from under the cart gripping the baby tightly as she leaped to freedom.

Mrs. Annie closed the door, wrapping the stolen keys in a towel under the cart, and hurried to get as far away from the scene as possible. Her nerves calmed as she passed several of the girls and no one seemed alarmed.

A half hour later, Boss left the lounge to make his rounds. Paulette jumped up, wiped the semen from her mouth, and shadowed her Daddy's every movement.

Boss was totally relaxed from the half-hour blow job he'd just had.

"Go down to the south wing and check on that problem child you brought in this house. See if the bitch is ready to get back to business!"

"Yes, Daddy." Paulette conceded.

While Paulette strolled off in the direction of the Queen's Quarters, Boss ran into one of his V.I.P clients. She unlocked the door and peeped inside looking for Cynthia, but there was no sight of the young woman. She walked in and removed the stun gun from her house coat, tipped over to the bed, and checked to see if Cynthia was underneath it, but there was still no sign of her. In panic mode, Paulette searched through the closets, in the bathroom and the window seal to see if it had been breached. Finding no sign of Cynthia, she rushed to alert Boss of her findings.

"Boss! Boss!" Paulette yelled hysterically.
Boss turned and looked in her direction with his forehead extended.

"Bitch, what the hell are you yelling for?"

"Daddy, she's not in her room!" Paulette replied.

"Did you check up under the bed?"

"I checked the entire room, including the widow seal. She might have chiseled her way out. There were no marks."

"Go down to the maid's quarters and get the baby. If the bitch is hiding in one of these rooms, she will be severely dealt with."

Boss stormed into the living room and got on the intercom. "I want every mutha fuckin' bitch in the house to stop what you're doing right now and report to the living room immediately! That's a direct order!" Within seconds, every woman in the residence, including the maid and the caretaker, nervously stood before the angry man. They were instructed to spread out to search high and low for the missing woman. Boss retreated to his room and shut the front office operation down until further notice. He wanted to make sure the problem child was found before anyone left the location. He headed back to the living room where he was met by Paulette.

"The baby's gone, too!" Paulette wailed, afraid that Boss would blame her.

Cynthia had broken his number one rule. Boss turned his attention to finding the disloyal party that helped them escape. He called an emergency meeting in the living room to get to the bottom of things. Every woman stood in a single file line. Boss entered the room clad in army gear, wielding a braided whip in his hand prepared to beat some ass.

"One of you bitches standing here before me today has betrayed me in the worst way possible! I'll be damned if we don't get to the bottom of which one of you bitches it was, right here and now!"

Boss went over to Paulette and slapped her to the ground.

"You brought the bitch in here! Did you get weak and decide to let her raggedy ass out?"

"Daddy, I was with you and ---"

"What in the hell does that mean? All you bitch's are slick as a can of oil!'"

Boss went from zero to ten studying their every move, searching for a sign of deception on any of the girls' faces. He paraded the entire line of working girls waiting for the guilty party to break. Surprisingly, everyone held their position. Boss forced each of the girls to the floor, face down. He started hitting them with the whip in the back and legs, causing the twisted strap to unravel. Enraged, he started feeling the back of their necks, checking for a rapid pulse. After he checked the last girl, he noticed how composed Mrs. Annie was.

"So it was your old ass who decided to betray my loyalty?" Boss questioned with an evil smirk on his face. He knew from the beat of each girls' pulse rate that none were nervous enough to have been guilty.

Caught off guard by Boss's inquisition, Mrs. Annie tried to explain away her involvement, but no words came out. It was as if her voice box had been shut off. She thought for sure that no one had seen her let Cynthia and the baby out. She looked over at the car-taker who shrugged her shoulders, then back at Boss with the letters G.U.I.L.T.Y written all over her puppy dog expression. It was if Mrs. Annie was a ventriloquist: her mouth moved but there were no sound at all.

"Take her to the basement and get the old bitch ready for the torture chamber." Boss instructed his bottom bitch.

Paulette hurried to her feet, grabbing the petrified old lady by the arm, and hauled her off to the basement. Mrs. Annie tried desperately to fight off her captor, but the arthritis in her left leg was no match for the younger and stronger Paulette. The other girls stood traumatized at the sight of the maid being taken away against her will. But no one dared to say a word.

"If I find out any of you bitches had a hand in helping to release one of my captives without my permission, you, too, will die." Boss walked off and not one of the girls budged an inch.

He got six paces up the hallway, snapped his fingers, and each of the girls promptly dispersed in single file order to their respective areas. He entered his private domain and went straight to the closet to suit up. Boss was determined to find out what Mrs. Annie knew about the disappearance of Cynthia, and how she was able to escape his confinement. He clad himself in all black, strapped on his steel-toed boots, and headed for the basement.

The doorbell rang and Boss stepped back into his room to get a visual of the monitor positioned on the front entrance. He paused for a minute seeing the two officers pacing back and forth in front of the camera. He rushed over to his walk-in closet, threw on his signature housecoat over his war outfit, and headed towards the front door. He had shut the front operation down so he was cool.

After a few minutes of talking to the officers, Boss invited both of them in for a complimentary blow job on the house to cover their troubles. The latter of the two officers stared intently at the steel-toed boots Boss was wearing, wondering what that was all about.

Cynthia was hospitalized and as a precautionary measure, the baby was taken in for a more thorough evaluation. For the first few days, Cynthia sat in the hot seat being questioned at length by several task force agents from the Special Victims Unit. They wanted to know about the prostitution going on inside the home. Cynthia gave a full account of every appointment, meeting and beating she endured at the hands of her captor. The agent called in a female detective to take several pictures of the partially healed scars on Cynthia's back, neck, arms, and legs. After, she tagged the photos and sent them to the evidence room.

"Ms. Barnes, is there anything else you can possibly think of that may help us in getting a better understanding of Mr. Bellefonte's operation?"

"I'm sorry, but I've told you all I know."

"Here's my card. If you think of anything else, don't hesitate to call me, no matter what time it is."

Where's my baby? Is she alright?"

"The baby was taken to pediatrics for a full examination. No worries at all, it's a procedure we take when victims are brought in with infant children. I'm sure you will have her back by morning."

For the rest of the evening, Cynthia sat in the heavily-guarded hospital room and cries through her emotions. She was dealing with the threat of her grandmother being admitted to an elderly home. Despite treatment, her cancer had grown, and her doctor had advised her to go to a hospice, since she had no family in town. Cynthia was confused by the actions of Paulette and how she had misled her. She once again felt abandon, deserted and lonely. She considered killing herself, but the thought of her precious daughter being without a mother and a father kept her alive, but dangerously close to the edge.

The next morning, the nurse entered the room with a breakfast tray in her hands.

"Ms. Barnes, here's some breakfast for you. Would you like me to turn on the television?"

"That's fine." Cynthia agreed, wanting to rid her mind of the terrible things Boss had done to her. Without Devon, her life had become unbearable.

"I'm going to redress your wraps and put new gauze on the wounds."

The nurse finished her duties, clicked on the television, and grabbed her clipboard from the wall. She filled in her time and headed to her next assignment.

Cynthia sat for a moment daydreaming, thinking of how naive she was not to have recognized the signs of Paulette and the pimp from the first day she arrived. She was thankful that Mrs. Annie had the nerve to do the right thing, but feared how Boss would react when he found out that she and the baby were gone. She knew the older woman would probably be spared, but worried about her being discovered as her accomplice.

Later that evening, the lead detective on the case showed up at her bedside holding a list of unanswered questions he had jotted down on a tablet.

"Ms. Barnes, how long would you say you were a resident in the house?"

"I was there for about seven months."

"While you were entertaining clients, where would your daughter be?"

"I told you before; I was only permitted to see Devianna for about a month the entire time I was there." Cynthia seemed confused as to why the agent had shifted his focus to her daughter and not on the mastermind.

"Why are you questioning me about my daughter? Is something wrong with her?"

"I'm sorry, Ms. Barnes, but after further investigation, the doctor has determined that the child was sexually molested on several occasions."

The echo of Cynthia's screams could be heard throughout the entire floor. She shook uncontrollably, eyes fixed on the policeman as if he had some sort of involvement in the sinister act. The emergency button was activated and several staff rushed in to tend to the out-of-control patient. She was strapped in a strait jacket, her hands bound for her own protection. After being injected with Tramadol, she was stabilized. The officer advised her that the baby would undergo further observation for the next few days and then be transferred to a specialist to determine the severity of the injuries.

A few days passed and a young blond from Child Protective Services arrived at Cynthia's bedside.

"Good morning, Ms. Barnes. How are you feeling today?"

"I've had better days," Cynthia responded slowly. Why are you here?"

"I'm from the office of Child Protective Services, and we understand that your baby has been molested," she said, handing her a business card.

"Yes. But she's getting treatment," Cynthia said nervously.

"Be that as it may, I'm here to advise you that your child will be taken into our custody upon release from the hospital. This is our routine procedure after an incident like this."

"No Ma'am! You can't do this to me! I would never hurt my baby!" Cynthia pleads.

"Ms. Barnes, there's nothing I can do to overturn the board's ruling. The decision was unanimous due to the severity of the child's case, and it's final."

"Listen, woman, as I explained to the agents, I had no control over my life in that house. Don't any of you understand what I went through? Or is it all about putting the blame on somebody?" Cynthia continued to plead her case on deaf ears.

"It may not have been your intention, but you had enough knowledge about the operation to know not to drag your daughter into that type of environment."

"Ma'am, a so-called friend of mine persuaded me to come to California. I'm from Ft. Worth, Texas. I had no knowledge at all of the type of environment I would be living in until weeks after I arrived. I would never have intentionally brought my daughter into that hell hole."

"Well, this should teach you a very valuable lesson, to always be aware of the people claiming to be your friends."

"But ma'am, please! Listen to me! You can't take my baby!"

"The decision is final, and there's nothing I can do about it. My hands are tied by the courts."

Cynthia begged and pleaded her case all the way up until the case worker left. A packet of documents were left behind for Cynthia to read over. She grabbed the packet off the sliding tray and stared at her daughter's name for a full four minutes without blinking. She was angry to realize that the document only left her with three options for her daughter's future.

1. Kiss her innocent baby girl one last time and send her into the waiting arms of an adoption agency rep.
2. Get a lawyer and take years sorting through the judicial system's

bull crap while the baby stayed in foster care.

3. Call Gran and get her to come and take the baby.

A glimmer of hope shone through as she thought about option three, but then she remembered how sick Gran was. Gran couldn't take care of anybody, not even herself.

And then there was Cynthia's own little secret, just in case all else failed.

She intently stared at the packet page by page until she had read the complete document. When she finished, she lay back on the bed, questioning the wisdom of the Almighty.

"God! What have I done to deserve this hell that I'm going through? I believed you when you said that you wouldn't put any more burdens on me than I could bear! Lord, I'm about to break! I can't take any more! Can you hear me? Show me a sign, Lord! Show me that you are who my Grandmother says you are!"

Cynthia's words grew louder as she continued to vent. The officer on duty entered the room and found the young woman with both hands stretched towards the ceiling, tears racing down her cheeks.

"Ma'am, are you okay?"

"Just leave me the hell alone! Please!" Cynthia answered, as if in a daze.

Seeing the woman's disgruntled state of mind he quickly left the room allowing her time alone. She grabbed the packet of adoption papers from the tray, and immediately her eyes fixed on the big bold letters that read, "Devianna Samantha Barnes."

"How can I live without my baby?" she thought. The only one who can help me is Gran. I've got to find some way to get to her.

One week later, Cynthia climbed out of the Peter built truck and thanked the driver. He had been so kind to give her a ride to Texas when she had no money. When she escaped from the hospital, there was no one she could call in California. She had tried to call Sam before she left, but Sam didn't answer. That's when she decided to run.

All she had to figure out now was how to get to her grandmother. With no money or clean clothes, her best bet was to find a shelter.

She remembered that Unity Park was on the south side, and the Salvation Army provided meals and shelter for the homeless there. The truck driver had let her off not too far from there, so she started walking.

It felt good to get a chance to shower and get a good night's sleep, but her dreams about her baby kept her tossing and turning. She wondered how she was adjusting and who she was with. She missed her so badly that she didn't think she could make it another day. But the thought of getting to Gran kept her going. She'd know what to do. With Gran's help, she'd be able to get Devianna back.

The next morning, the clerk at the shelter helped her find the location of the James M. West Hospice Center. She arranged a ride for her with Mec-a-Bus, and told her she was welcome to come back that night. As hard as the staff tried to cheer her up, Cynthia's spirit was low. She had no idea what to expect when she went to see Gran.

"Good morning, May I help you," the nurse behind the window asked.

"I'm here to see my grandmother, Miss Wanda Pearl Powell."

"Oh, yes. Miss Powell will be so glad to see you. She hasn't had any visitors since she's been here.

Cynthia's heart dropped at the thought of her grandmother being abandoned by the rest of the family. She must have wondered where she was and why she hadn't heard from her in so long.

"If you'll follow me, I'll take you to her room. But I have to warn you, she's not doing too well these days. She doesn't remember anyone and she have lost a lot of weight. We're trying to get her to eat, but she's a stubborn little lady, so we have to feed her intravenously. I'm sure that your visit will do her a world of good."

Cynthia's stomach was turning as the nurse pushed the door open. After losing her baby, she felt as if she just couldn't take any more. When she looked at the frail, shrunken body lying in the bed, she had to fight hard to hold back the tears.

This didn't look anything like her grandmother. She thought, for a second, that she was in the wrong room.

"Miss Powell, you have a visitor," the nurse said.

The figure in the bed turned towards Cynthia and smiled, tears rolling down her wrinkled cheeks.

The tears were contagious. They fell freely from Cynthia's eyes as she approached the bed and squeezed her grandmother's hand, as the nurse walked out to give them time alone.

"Gran, I'm here. This is me, Cynthia."

The little old lady looked her in the eye. "I've been waiting for you," she replied.

"I'm so sorry I haven't been her, Gran. I got here as soon as I could."

"I know, Baby. All that's important is that you're here now. I've been missing' you, too."

"How are you feeling, Gran? Are you hurting anywhere?

The pain comes and goes. You never can tell about cancer. I think it's getting' the best of me."

"No, Gran. Don't think like that. You've got to fight it. I'll help you."

"No, Baby. My fight is over. I've turned it over to the good Lord, now. I'm ready."

"Please don't say that! You can't go! Please, God! Don't let this happen!"

"It's not up to me, now, is it?"

The knot in Cynthia's stomach was turning into a sharp pain as she realized the hopelessness of the situation. Her grandmother's face was pale, and her breathing labored. Cynthia felt as if she was losing her at that very moment.

Gran was trying desperately to say something else, and Cynthia could almost make out the word, "baby" from her parched lips. But after the first syllable, she coughed and exhaled. It was the last breath she would ever take.

"No, Gran! No! Don't go! I need you!"

But Cynthia realized her cries were hopeless, and Gran had waited for her to say good-bye before she died. Once again, a sense of emptiness enveloped her body.

Hearing the sobs from the room, the nurse peeked in again, walked over to her patient, and felt for a pulse. Realizing that the end had come, she turned to Cynthia and said, "I'm so sorry. She's gone." The nurse reached towards her grandmother's face, patted her cheek gently, and closed her eyes.

A sense of panic gripped Cynthia and she charged out of the room, sobbing hysterically. When she got to the end of the hall, she stopped and slid down to the floor, feeling that she had finally lost everything good in her life. All hope of any kind of happiness, of getting her baby back, of having a family, all was lost.

Cynthia began to second-guess her purpose in life and within minutes, she lost any reason she may have had to go on. She simply lost the will to live. Reaching for the scissors the nurse left on the cart beside her, she snapped. Cynthia bolted to the nearest bathroom, locking the door to the stall, and slashed at the skin guarding the arteries in her wrist. Blood slowly seeped from the open wounds until the second round of self- inflicted cuts were administered. Cynthia dug deep into the freshly opened wounds and the blood flow escalated.

"Maybe you will answer me now, Lord," Cynthia pleaded. As the words rolled off her tongue, she passed out.

Chapter 7

Samantha woke up to find Leon's side of her bed completely deserted. She wiped her eyes and glanced over her shoulder to check the time. Immediately, her antennas emerged when she saw 4:37 in bold red numbers. Since she'd allowed Leon in her home to shack up, it was highly unlikely for the lawyer to be up and about his daily routine doing anything before his first cup of coffee. Sam eased out of the bed, crept up to the closet, and grabbed her night gown. She wrapped her naked body and proceeded up the hallway looking for Leon, pausing at the light barely visible from the front office. She tipped to the door, pressed her ear against it, and listened to the conversation.

"Bob, I'll try to get up there to see Mr. Jordan on Monday evening, if possible. Oh, by the way, his wife transferred the half a million over to the off shore account last night. I'm scheduled to meet with her at the office this morning to go over the "discovery of evidence" motion the secretary filed on behalf of the defendants."

Silence fell momentarily.

"I just don't think it's wise to talk about anything other than the case when visiting any of the defendants. There are way too many listening ears and watching eyes at the jailhouse. Let's see if I can get him to tell me where it's hidden in a "morning prayer" huddle inside the courtroom on the 15th. It's a much safer environment and the ideal place for me anyway.

Leon promptly ended the call and placed his phone on the desk. He sat staring at the paperwork, and then tossed it into his briefcase. He hit the dimmer switch and returned to the bedroom where he found Sam snoring under the covers.

"Samantha. Samantha!" He was slightly annoyed because he knew Sam was a light sleeper. Maybe she was trying to avoid his attention.

"Yes, Daddy," she mumbled as she covered her yawn." What time is it?" Sam turned over and wiped her eyes.

"It's breakfast time." The lawyer replied.

"Babe, it's ten till five. Why are you up so early?" Sam asked with a frown.

"I have to get to the office, meet with a few people, and make a few calls."

"Damn! Why so early? Who in the hell are you calling? The Godfather of the Mafia or somebody?" Sam threw the down comforter off and rolled out of the bed.

Leon frowned, confused as to where and when she had put on a gown.

"Well, I'll be damned! You sleep ready to roll?" Leon asked, unwilling to let the night gown go unnoticed. He knew Sam would always come to bed in the same manner she entered into the world.

"I thought you knew. I stay ready to keep from having to get ready." Samantha winked and closed the bathroom door behind her.

The United States of America vs. Thomas Jordan and his thirteen co-defendants got under way on March 15, 2006. Samantha sat in the front row in support of the defense team, while she was excited to see how Leon would challenge the Federal Government. She kept the high-frequency pen on high pitch, in hopes of catching an earful. On the first day of the hearing, Attorney Hale was overheard telling his clients the government offered one of their co-defendants immunity in the case in exchange for information leading to the fifteen million dollars and the ringleader's hidden accounts.

On the third day, all twelve defendants and the lawyers were huddled together with their heads bowed low on a false pretense of prayer. Sam was on top of her game. After obtaining the information she'd come for, Sam turned her attention to the prosecutor's side and accidently stumbled upon the location where the informant and his family were hiding out. She waited patiently until the court recessed for lunch, and eased out the courtroom with Jonetta close on her trail.

Sam listened to the location of the money over and over in her head to make sure it was embedded in her memory. The trial was postponed while both sides prepared to proceed. Sam knew she had to act fast because once the snitch's testimony hit the stand, Ernie and his people were doomed.

Later that evening, Samantha rode by her old stomping grounds to see if any of the known killers, were still lurking the streets for work. She pulled up, jumped out of the car, and made her way to the back of the "Jets." As she searched throughout the walkways, she paused and looked up at the boarded apartment Jonathan, Clef and the GNB boys once called their headquarters. She knew with many of the youngsters that hung out up there, a 187 wasn't but a call away. As she turned to walk away, she paused and looked over her shoulder at the apartment, threw two fingers to the sky, and pounded them against her breast in memory of the fallen soldier. There was no chance of bringing Lil Jonathan back from the grave, but Clef was a totally different story.

Sam walked back to the front parking area and returned to her car, eyes fixed on the apartment she once shared with Jonetta and Mama Dee. Tears began to trickle down her face as vivid images of her mother standing at the front door smoking a cigarette resurfaced in her mind. Sam was lost without the guidance of the one who owned the game. She wiped her face with the back of her hand and put in a call to D Roc. She knew D Roc wasn't a killer, but she realized long ago that he was well connected to the hit men.

The phone rang several times before a deep voice bellowed into the line. "Sam! What's good?" D Roc greeted her.

"Oh nothing too much, Just rolling through checking on you. What you got going on?"

"Back here lying low, grinding as usual."

"Come up to the front."

"Are you up there at Mama Dee's apartment? Damn! I'm tripping for real. I apologize. It doesn't seem like Mama Dee or the little homie is gone. My bad, my peoples, I didn't mean no harm."

"It's cool, Roc. I know Mama's hard to forget. I'm sitting in the car in front of our old spot thinking about her and Li'l

Jonathan."

"Give me a minute."

D Roc showed up ten minutes later. He jumped in the Benz and hugged his old friend around the neck.

"Roc, I have a problem that requires some urgent attention."

"Just say the word, Sam, and I can make it happen."

"I need to get rid of a witness."

"A government witness?" D Roc said with excitement in his voice.

"Yeah. And I'm talking about in a few days or less."

"Damn! That's not going to be easy. Besides, they'll give your ass a million years for fucking with one of them snitches."

"If you scared, Baby Boy, get out the way."

D Roc opened the door and told Sam he wasn't scared of anything. It was just certain things he wasn't into dealing with, and messin' with the feds was the main one. He slammed the door behind him, pulled out a cigarette and hurriedly walked away.

Sam rode around for an hour thinking of how to get her problem solved until she decided to stop stressing and head over to her cousin's place. Sam drove to the Mira Vista Homes and pulled into Jonetta's driveway. She wanted to get some sort of confirmation on making Clef's bond or planning his escape, but no one was at the Barnes' residence. She started walking towards her cousin Vonda's house when her cell phone rang.

"Hey, Babe," Sam answered.

"Are you at the house?" Leon asked.

"No. I made a quick stop to check on my cousin, Vonda."

"Okay. I'll be home a little later. I have a few things I need to take care of when I leave the office."

"So I guess I'll see you when you get home."

"It won't be too late."

Sam rang the bell and Marcus responded by opening the door.

"Hey, Sam! What's good?"

"That sausage you been holding for hostage," Sam joked.

"Come on in. Vonda's in the kitchen."

"Yeah, that's what I thought with your scary ass."

Sam entered the home and maneuvered her way to the kitchen laughing.

"Hey, Cuz."

"Hello, Sam! What are you doing out this way?"

"I came through to discuss some business with Jonetta, but she wasn't home. I called and told her I was coming up this way to check on you. I just wanted to talk with my cousin for a few minutes, if that's alright with you."

"Sam, you are my family, and nothing could ever take away the love I have for you," Vonda said sincerely.

Sam winced at the pang of guilt she felt after having slept with her cousin's husband.

Marcus grabbed the dominoes off the shelf and challenged Sam to a few games for money. A couple of hours passed before Trevon and Jonetta showed up. They came right over when they saw Sam's car in their driveway. They all had a few drinks. Trevon called into Carson to see if he and Ingrid would join them, but Carson declined, explaining that Ingrid had been called into work at the last minute.

"All right, then. I'll see you at the studio in the morning."

"Cool," Carson replied, and he hung up.

Marcus invited everyone up to the top floor to see the expensive upgrades in his theatre room. There was a ticket box with a mannequin inside, a popcorn stand, and another mannequin stood at the front entrance to the door.

"This is really nice, man" Trevon said.

"Thanks, my man. I ended up having to fork out forty G's on this room alone."

"Damn, Marcus! You back rolling for real!" Sam hollers out.

"Oh, Sam, that little loss I took was a minor setback waiting on a major get back." Marcus replied with authority.

Vonda put her arms around her man and kissed him squarely on the lips. She was thankful Marcus was able to regroup financially, and was now keeping the large sums of money in their bank account as normal people did. The party moved on to the game room and began to shoot pool, drink shots and talk shit until almost midnight, when Samantha's cell phone rang.

"Yawl holds the noise down. It's my baby calling."

"Exactly, which one of them is it?" Marcus interrupted with a slur.

Sam answered the phone and pointed at him with a dirty look.

"Hey babe, what's going on?"

"I thought it was some dinner going on, but I see you're still out and about having a good time from what I hear in the background." Leon complained.

"It's almost midnight and you're just now wondering where your dinner is?"

"Truthfully speaking, I was wondering where my woman was this late at night."

"Oh, my! That's a first, me hearing anything about her."

"Where are you?"

"I told you I was going by my cousin's."

"Yes, but you didn't say shit about spending the night."

"I didn't realize it was so late until the phone rang and the time flashed on the screen. I'm getting ready to leave here now. See you in a minute."

"Yeah, we'll see. Maybe something else will come up along the way."

"Bye-ee," Sam cooed as she ended the call.

Samantha was amazed at how Leon was trying to handle her. She had never been reprimanded by the lawyer and didn't plan on letting him get away with it now. She gathered her things, said goodbye to her friends and family, and stumbled down the block with Jonetta close behind. Sam gave her sister a hug, jumped in the Benz, and backed out of the driveway.

Sam was half-way home when her cell phone rang. She rumbled through her purse until her right hand found the lighted object. Not recognizing the number, she frowned and threw it on the seat beside her. The phone promptly rang again. Seeing the number a second time, Sam answered with impatience in her voice.

"Hello!"

"Sam, this is Ingrid. You need to get to the hospital ASAP. It's about Cynthia. She's in critical condition."

The many shots of Crown Sam had just consumed immediately wore off. She sat at the light speechless.

"Are you there, Sam?"

"Yeah, I'm on my way. Where's the baby?

"Cynthia's been in surgery ever since I made it in to work, and I haven't seen anyone else."

"I'm in route now."

Sam hung up and quickly called Trevon to tell him the news. The phone rang several times before he answered.

"What's up Sam?"

"I found her."

"You found who?"

"Cynthia. She's at Baylor Hospital. Meet me there as soon as possible."

"Baylor? Isn't that where Ingrid works?"

"Yeah. Come on."

"Where's the.........?"

Sam hung up missing the last of Trevon's questions and raced towards the hospital. She arrived in fifteen minutes flat, parked, and rushed to the emergency room entrance. She was met by a teary-eyed Ingrid.

"What's going on?" Sam demanded.

"When I got to work, I was called in to surgery. It was a suicide attempt and she was bleeding out. When I scrubbed and went in to the operating room, I couldn't believe what I saw. It was Cynthia!

"Cynthia? What happened? How'd she get back here?"

"I don't know how she got back, but when the police found her, she had slit her wrist and she was bleeding to death. She was immediately taken to surgery. She's lost a lot of blood. Doctors are working now to stabilize the bleeding. It's not looking good though. She has deep lacerations and it appears as if she may have tried to take her own life by severing a main artery." Ingrid explained.

"Is she going to make it?"

"I'm not sure, but if she doesn't get a blood transfusion in time, she will definitely........"

The intercom blared, "Code red! Code red! Team Black to I.C.U!" abruptly interrupting the conversation.

"I have to go answer this call. I'll be back as soon as I can. Stay here and I'll keep you posted." Ingrid told Sam before jogging off towards the elevator.

A few minutes passed and the first of Sam's crew arrived. Trevon bailed out of his car at the front entrance of the emergency room while Jonetta parked. He quickly located Sam steadily pacing the floor.

"What's up, Sam? Where are Cynthia and the baby?"

"Ingrid came down a few minutes ago and said she was still in surgery."

"What's the room number?"

"I don't know, but you can't go into the operating room."

Jonetta parked and came through the door looking around.

"Here we are, Sis." Samantha yelled out from a few feet away.

"What's going on? Where are Cynthia and the baby?" Jonetta asked.

"Cynthia's in surgery, Ingrid said, and I don't know where the baby is."

"She's in surgery for what?"

"Ingrid said something about Cynthia supposedly slit her wrist."

"She slit her wrist? It 'ain't that much going on in the world, for a person to try to off themselves!" Jonetta quipped with a frown.

"I knew she was in some kind of trouble." Trevon chimed in as hit the wall in anger.

"Babe, calm down. Everything is going to be alright." Jonetta tried to assure her husband.

"No! It's all my fault! I didn't see about Cynthia like Devon asked me to!" Trevon sobbed uncontrollably. He fell against the wall and slid down to the ground.

Samantha walked over to the information station to ask about Cynthia.

"Ma'am, I don't see anyone by the name of Cynthia Powell in our system."

"Jonetta, isn't Cynthia's last name Powell?" Sam yelled.

"As far as I know, it's Cynthia Kristine Powell."

"She's saying there's no one in her system by that name."

"I don't know then. Try Barnes, she may have taken Big Twin's name and we didn't know about it." Jonetta said, walking over to join Sam in her search for Cynthia.

"I doubt that very seriously, because if Big Twin and Cynthia got married, I'd be the first to know.

The attendant typed in Barnes and the name "Cynthia K. Barnes" popped up.

"Here she is. Mrs. Cynthia Kristine Barnes. She's in surgery at the moment."

"I didn't know they got married and obviously you didn't either, Sam." Jonetta whispered to Sam with a menacing grin on her face.

Samantha turned to inform Trevon of Cynthia's status and the elevator opened up. Ingrid slowly exited with her head hung low. Sam moved towards her to get an update and Ingrid shook her head in disbelief while she desperately tried to fight back the tears.

"Dr. Meshito did everything he could to save her life, but her body was just too weak to endure the second surgery it required to get the transfusion working properly. She didn't make it. I'm so sorry! They pronounced her dead at 3:46 A.M. The timing hit Trevon like a ton of bricks. It was the precise timing Devon was pronounced dead, according to the police report. Trevon backed up holding his heart and gasping for air until his body deflated and he hit the floor. Ingrid rushed over to check his pulse.

"I need some help over here. Can someone please get me a gurney?" Ingrid yelled out.

"Trevon. Trevon! Trevon! Wake up, Baby! Please wake up!"

Jonetta screamed hovering over Ingrid's back.

A male nurse pushed a gurney over and Trevon was lifted on top and rushed off to an exam room. Jonetta kept pace with the hospital bed every step of the way, praying his illness hadn't once again inflamed. Ingrid raced to get the unconscious man checked into a room for diagnosis. She waited for the doctor to arrive before leaving to go find Samantha. Within minutes of Ingrid's emergency page, the doctor arrived, checked his pulse and started an I.V. He drew blood and checked for clots. Once the doctor completed his initial observation, he gave his diagnosis.

"Until the lab results are clear, I can only say that the patient has hyperventilated, causing the brain to shut down on the nervous system. He needs plenty of fluids and lots of rest."

"What caused this?"

"It's generally caused by built-up stress, but it could be a multitude of things. We'll just have to wait until the lab results come back"

"Has he been worrying a lot lately?" Ingrid asked.

"Stress can inflame a variety of ailments already contracted in the body," the doctor said looking Jonetta directly in the face. He scribbled on the clip board and left the room.

Jonetta leaned over and kissed Trevon on the forehead. Exhausted from the night of boozing, she flopped down in the seat next to the bed to rest her eyes, all the while holding onto Ingrid's hand.

"It's going to be alright, Babe. You're a warrior and a fighter. Now is not the time to give up."A single tear rolled from Trevon's right eye.

Now that Trevon was situated, Jonetta vowed not to leave his side. Meanwhile, Ingrid went to look for Sam. She stopped at the information station and paged her friend to come to the fifth floor. A few minutes later, Sam arrived and the two headed in the direction of Cynthia's surgery. When they got to the doorway, Sam halted at the front entrance. She inhaled a deep gasp of air, desperately trying to gain control of her fragile state of mind. Ingrid grabbed her trembling hand and began to pray. By the time she finished, Sam had mustered up the courage to deal with reality. She turned the corner into the recovery room, fighting back the tears. Ingrid moved closer to the body and pulled the sheet from her face. Sam batted her long lashes to fight back the tears, now welling up in her eyes. Cynthia's lifeless body was much too overwhelming for her to process. After minutes of staring at her childhood friend, the reality set in and she realized the Double Dutch Queen was gone forever. Sam's hardened surface broke, and the tears rushed down her cheeks like a faucet. She had never experienced the hurt she was going through for anyone else besides her mother and Big Twin. Ingrid wrapped her arm around Sam's shoulder and whispered in her ear.

"This is why it's a must that we get our lives in order with Christ today, before it's too late, Sam."

Sam stared at Ingrid, and then back down at Cynthia. Unable to keep her emotions in check any longer, Sam wiped the tears from her face and the snot from her runny nose and lashed out.

"Don't bring God into this now!" she spurted out, glaring at Ingrid.

She turned back to the still body on the gurney. "Cynthia, I will find out who did this to you! Who drove you to kill yourself, my beautiful friend? You just rest your soul in Paradise, and I promise to handle the rest of your troubles here on earth."

Still in shock, Sam departed the room with her head down and her spirit low. The body of Cynthia lying dormant on the gurney with her eyes wide open would forever register in the back of her mind. Ingrid stayed behind and prayed for Cynthia's soul before leaving the room and catching up with Sam, now half-way down the hall. She reached for Sam's hand, but Sam, now belligerent, screamed at the top of her lungs.

"Whoever did this to Cynthia will pay with their fucking life?"

Ingrid wrapped her arms around her friend and tried to console her, but it was much too late for talking with Sam. The damage was done.

Ingrid approached the first information station she saw and

paged Jonetta.

"Say, Christi, can you look up Trevon Barnes for me? Please see if he's been put into the system yet."

"Yes, I sure can. What's the last name again?"

"Barnes. His first name is Trevon."

The desk clerk scrolled through the list of patients with the last name of Barnes and only found Cynthia Powell Barnes.
"He hasn't been admitted into the system as of yet. He may still be in an E.R. intake room."

"How about paging for Jonetta Barnes again? Have her meet me at the emergency entrance."

"Will do.

"Thanks, girl. I'll talk to you later. Come on, Sam. Let's make our way to the entrance of the E.R. so we can meet up with Jonetta."

As the two walked off, Sam turned to ask Ingrid a question. "Say, Ingrid. I know you see this kind of thing every day, but are it that easy for you to view dead bodies and just think nothing about it?"

"It's not that it's easy, Sam. After seeing so much death here at the hospital, I realize the pain Cynthia may have endured in her short life is now over. I just wish she hadn't taken her own life. There's no forgiveness for that, Sam. So as much as she may have been brought up to believe in the Resurrection, she gave it all away with one irresponsible decision."

Sam knew full well what Ingrid was talking about. Since being released from prison, her friend had come a long way. And although Jonetta had been the mastermind of many of their scams, Ingrid was the most intelligent one by far. The two interlocked arms and stepped into the elevator. When the doors opened, Jonetta was standing at the entrance to the E.R.

"Hey, Sis! Where's Trevon? Is he ok?" Samantha asked.

"He's in the same room and yes, he's doing just fine. The doctor says he over exerted himself and it may have been stress-related."

"I'll go check on him." Ingrid said.

"The doctor says he needs plenty of rest. He went ahead and admitted him for a 24-hour observation. He said something about making sure he's getting enough oxygen to his brain. Where's Cynthia's body?"

"We just came from seeing her. She's in a room on the fifth floor outside surgery." Sam replied.

"They'll probably take her to the morgue soon," Ingrid added.

"Your eyes are bloodshot, Sis. It looks like you've been crying."

"I have. I just can't believe she's gone."

"Once the coroner is finished with the autopsy, how long will it take for the body to be released?" Jonetta asked.

"I can get it tagged for pick-up as soon as the medical examiner releases the body. All I need to know is what funeral home to call." Ingrid replied.

"Ok, I'll wait to see her at the funeral."

"Why don't you two go to the house and get some rest? I'll keep watch on Trevon throughout my shift."

"I wish I would leave his side for more than a few minutes. If he wakes up and doesn't see my face, his spoiled ass will have a panic attack."

"Come on, Sis. You need some rest, too. I'll spend the night at your house and we can get up early in the morning to head back."

"Ingrid, you need to call me right away if he happens to wake up. I can rush back up here and act like I went to Mc Donald's or something. I just don't want him to be trippin' like I abandoned him. He has a real problem with that from the way his father did them."

"I will call you the moment I see him move." Ingrid responded as she laughed.

Early the next morning before sunrise, the girls were headed to the hospital. Samantha entered the parking lot and found Carson parked in the patient's pick-up area. His seat was reclined and a jacket covered his upper body, blocking the light.

"Carson! Carson! Samantha yelled as she tapped on the window.

Startled, Carson abruptly moved and peeped over the top of his jacket. Surprised to see Sam, Carson lowered the window to hear her conversation.

"What's going on, Carson?"

"Damn! You knocked on the window like you the police!"

"Why are you up here so early?"

"I've been up since 2:30 this morning. Trevon called last night and talked my ear off."

"He wasn't supposed to know Jonetta left the hospital."

"He wasn't sweating that. He said she needed some rest."

Jonetta proceeded towards the front of the hospital with Samantha and Carson not far behind. When she entered the room, Trevon's eyes opened wide at the sight of his wife.

"There goes my baby! Oh, girl. Look at you! You don't know how good it feels to call you my girl." Trevon crooned.

"Babe, stop it! We ran into Carson in the parking lot. I guess you already knew I went home last night." Jonetta added.

When Carson and Samantha entered the room, Trevon stared him down for a few seconds.

"What's wrong man? Why you got the big eye on me like that?"

"You talk too much. That's what's wrong."

"Man, I apologize. I didn't know shit was a secret," Carson replied and shrugged his shoulders.

"No sweat, my peoples. It's all good. You know we down like four flat tires without a spare, and that's for life.

Trevon turned to Jonetta and asked, "Did anybody find out what happened to Cynthia? Why would she kill herself?"

"I didn't even know she was back in town," Sam replied.

"I didn't, either," Trevon continued. "That's what I was paying the P.I. to find out. If he'd done his job, maybe this wouldn't have happened."

"I never understood what could drive a person to kill himself. Hell! Cynthia had a baby to look after!" Sam chimed in.

"Where is the baby? Does anybody know?" Trevon asked.

Sam replied, "When I first got here, Ingrid said there was no sign of the baby. Maybe something happened to Devianna and that's what drove her to do this."

"I don't know. But we sho' as hell need to find out. That's family.

"Sho' ya right," echoed Trevon.

Carson leaned over the bedrail, gave his cousin a hug, and handed him the clothing from off the back of the lazy boy.

Trevon disappeared into the restroom, slipped into his pants, and approached the mirror to wash his face. He stared at himself in disbelief as he noticed his striking resemblance to the late Parnell Jenkins. The wrinkles in his forehead had become a permanent fixture on his face. He was as worried as he was the day he found out his father's true identity. Would his own face be a constant reminder of the reason he went to prison? Or maybe even worse his brother's killer?

"I'm ready," he said, as he stepped back into the hospital room. Is Cynthia's body still available for viewing?"

"No. It's in the morgue. Has the doctor released you yet?" Jonetta demanded.

"Don't you think it's a little late to be asking him that when he's dressed and apparently ready to make his escape?" Samantha joked.

"Calm down. The doctor came through earlier and everything checked out just fine. He advised me to at least get some rest since I was already in the system." Trevon responded, lying through his teeth. "Can I see Cynthia before I leave this hospital?"

"Babe she's already been transferred to the morgue.

"He was making sure you paid that overnight residency fee they so conveniently tally up in that high ass hospital bill you'll get in the mail in a couple of weeks," Carson quipped to lighten the mood.

"Breakfast is on me, folks!" he continued. Let me call Ingrid and see if she can join us."

"Oh, shit!" Samantha snapped, suddenly realizing she hadn't spoken to Leon since she was supposed to be home in a few minutes several hours ago.

"I know he's probably pissed off but oh well, family comes before a fuck any day!" she continued as she dug around in her purse for her phone. She keyed in his number and the phone rang several times, but there was no answer. She tried again and it went straight to voice mail.

"Carson, were you able to reach Ingrid?" Jonetta asked.

"She didn't answer. She's either in the shower or out like a light."

"Well, I guess it's just the four of us. Can we go to Mimi's in the Highlands?'

"That's cool. Babe. I'm going to roll with Carson. I need to talk to him about a few things."

Jonetta agreed but she was caught off guard by his request. She considered Trevon to be her friend, partner and husband in all aspects of life. He was her rock through the tough times and she was the same for him. Her mind wandered, wondering what was only deserving of Carson's ear. She hoped he wasn't going bad and discussing their secret.

"Okay, Babe. We'll meet you at the restaurant."
Jonetta entered the parking garage, looking around until she located the Jaguar. She paid the overnight fee and rolled out, trailing Sam.

Twenty minutes later, the four were seated at a booth by the window discussing a proper burial for the Double-Dutch Queen.

"Carson, you need to see if Ingrid can check the paperwork and see if there's a next of kin to contact. Her family needs to know she's passed and we desperately need to find the baby before it's too late." Trevon said.

"Yeah. See if there's anything in the paperwork that has her last address on file. I have a real live plan." Samantha added.

"We need to get the address of the Chocolate Swirl from the private investigator and work from the inside." Trevon suggested.

"That's what I'm talking about! I'm cool with that. California, here we come! The triple threat is in effect." Samantha cheered.

"Carson, you stay behind and keep things rolling on this end. We're going out to California and there ain't no telling how long we'll be out there. I'll call you if shit gets funky."

"That's cool. Just don't get me caught up with a prison

sentence again."

"I can assure you that won't happen again. This time around,

"Get you some rest so you can be powered up when you head out west. They say them Cali boys be on some real gangster shit."

"That's the way I like it."

"I got your back one hundred percent and then some. If you need extra muscle, don't hesitate to call me."

"I have all the muscle and mind controls I need in these two dangerous mutha fuckas right here." Trevon pointed to the two women at the table.

Carson knew his folks were all-in girls that would always be loyal and down for the cause.

Cynthia's death was ruled a suicide. Her body was tagged and transferred to Spencer's Funeral Home to be prepared for a date with the undertaker. On the morning of the funeral, Trevon sat on the edge of the bed, sick to his stomach with his head resting in his hands. Jonetta entered the bedroom and saw the look on his face. Concerned, she asked him what was wrong.

"Trevon, are you okay?" Jonetta asked.

"I'm cool, other than the fact that I feel like I let Devon down."

"Babe, you can't hold on to that guilt forever. All we can do is send Cynthia off right and get about our mission to find the baby. She chose to go out like she did and there's nothing we can do about it but get the baby home safe."

Jonetta grabbed his hand and pulled him to her. They held on tight for a few moments, grateful for each other's love. They finished dressing and left for the church.

Because Trevon considered Cynthia his sister-in-law, accompanied by the guilt he was now struggling with, he held back no expenses and sent the young mother off in style. She truly did look like she was sleeping. Cynthia was dressed to the hilt in a black and white pants suit with a crisp white blouse. Her white casket was covered with a huge bouquet of yellow roses, and pink and white wreaths adorned each side. Her beauty made her dying so young even more tragic. The news of Cynthia's death had crushed her spirit, taking its toll on her heart. So besides a few of her church members, and a handful of childhood friends of the

"Double Dutch Queen" from the Jets, there were not many in attendance. The family section was filled by Trevon, Jonetta, Ingrid, Carson, Sam, and Leon. Under the circumstances, Leon had forgiven Sam for staying out all night without calling, and joined the grievers.

The funeral was so sad. The eulogy was read by a teary-eyed Trevon and the choir sang "Going up yonder," leaving not a dry eye in God's house. The pastor gave an inspiring sermon about suicide, how we all commit our own suicide when we don't live up to our potential. He ended with a prayer that all in the church would accept God's will with grace. Cynthia was escorted from the funeral to her final resting place in a beautiful white carriage pulled by two pearl-white stallions.

Chapter 8

In the days following the funeral, Trevon paced the floor dragging his feet in deep depression. The burden of Cynthia being caught up in something so detrimental that it would cause her to take her own life weighed like a ton of bricks on his mind. He picked up the phone and called the one person he felt he could talk to as a son. Ironically, the former Mrs. Jenkins had been more like a mother to him than his own had been since he was released from prison. She advised him to be careful, to watch his back, and not to overplay his hand to the enemy. He guessed she had learned a few things from her husband, the man who both gave him his life and ruined it.

Early Friday morning, Trevon put in a call to Sam to remind her of the Monday morning departure. She assured him that she'd be at the airport on time and ready to roll. She hung up the phone and decided to spend the weekend making sure Leon was properly taken care of. The couple dined in on Saturday and Sunday. Sam put in her best work both in the kitchen and in the bedroom, leaving nothing to the sexual imagination of her boo. Leon was hooked on her performance. He hated to see her leave. He made sure she knew he had her back and if anything legal needed to happen, he'd be on a plane to rescue her and her friends.

Leon arrived at DFW Airport in time for Sam to check in and get in line to board her flight. She leaned over and gave the lawyer a quick peck on the cheek before getting out of the car.

"Babe, please don't forget to see if TJ wants me to get that little problem taken care of for him.

"I'll get a chance to visit with him later this evening to discuss the case," Leon said as he rolled his eyes upward. "And I will make sure he knows his ex has his best interests in mind."

"No need to get jealous, Honey. This is about business, not pleasure." Sam replied. She leaned in and gave him a long, lingering kiss to remove any doubts he may have had about her relationship with TJ. She closed the door behind her, blew him a kiss, and smiled. She put a little extra swing in her hips as she sashayed to the entrance of the airport.

When Sam arrived at the baggage check-in, she was confronted by a flirtatious Rasta baggage clerk with long dreads. He moved around her as if he were listening to a bumping reggae beat that nobody else could hear.

"Damn! What man allows such a beautiful rose the leisure time to travel alone?" The Rasta asked with a strong Jamaican accent.

"Look here, Brother Man, all that you talking about are quite flattering, but unless you plan to board the flight with me to California, I guess I'll see you next lifetime. Right now, I'm on a bloody mission."

"Well can I at least have your number?" The baggage man asked while tagging her suitcases.

"You sure in the hell can. Its 817-777-9311" Sam yelled back as she moved towards her boarding gate. Excited to get the digits, the Rasta wrote the number down and put the torn piece of paper in his pocket.

"Too easy," thought Sam as she sped up towards the gate.

Sam boarded the flight and took her seat beside the small framed window. Within minutes, an older white gentleman slowly paced the aisle diligently searching for an accurate match to his ticket. Sam's eyes bucked as the man moved into her sight line. She flung her blazer over her head and leaned against the window pretending to be asleep. The man came to a halt next to where she was sitting, and loaded his briefcase in the storage area above. Sam peeped out from the jacket to see what was going on, but quickly ducked back inside when she saw him standing over her. He took the seat beside her, belted himself in, and prepared for takeoff. Once everyone boarded and the plane began to move, the man tapped her on the arm to remind her to buckle her seatbelt, but Sam didn't budge.

"Excuse me, Ma'am. You may want to buckle up. We're getting ready for takeoff."

Sam used her head like a lamp stand and shifted the jacket on top, keeping her face plastered to the coat like blanket. She reached underneath and buckled her seatbelt in silence.

Her silence continued through the two-hour flight. She could not allow her seatmate to hear her voice. When the plane landed, the mysterious woman stayed put until all the passengers were off. She gathered her things and wiped the sweat from her brow. Strolling up the ramp with eyes glued on the people waiting to board, Sam eased her way to the rental car pick-up station where she encountered two officers questioning a desk clerk. She darted into the restroom and locked herself in a stall, crouching on a toilet seat with both feet out of sight. After thirty long minutes of kneeling on the toilet lid, Sam exited the restroom with a scarf draped across her face and headed for the baggage claim, visibly shaken by the fact that she'd almost been caught by Ringhauser, the man she sat next to on the plane.

She had taken his credit cards and Rolex a year before, leaving him stranded in a hotel.

After that close call at the airport, Samantha was well overdue for the promise of the California sun. After calling Leon to let him know she had arrived safely, she treated herself to a massage at the hotel spa. And by sunset, Sam was lounging in the hot tub at the Holiday Inn Suite, enjoying some much needed rest and relaxation.

By the time the weekend arrived, Sam was antsy from being in the hotel room for days, awaiting the arrival of her two friends. On the third day, Sam slipped on a bathing suit and headed out to the pool area to await the call that the others were ready to be picked up. As soon as she left the building, she was assaulted by the heat of the day. When she felt the sweat forming behind her knees and in her cleavage, her body instinctively made a U-turn back into the building. She decided the cool of the air conditioning was better than sweating her hair back.

"Damn! It's scorching out there!" she mumbled to herself.

She unlocked the door to the suite and lay across the bed contemplating her next move. The memory of her and Big Twin's secret rendezvous lingered deep in her consciousness until it angered her spirit. She remembered being pregnant by Devon, now dead for five years, and being threatened by him to abort the child. She was mentally prepared to find out where the baby was and she was more determined than ever to find out what drove Cynthia to suicide. Within minutes, the heat of the sun and the exhaustion of her memories lulled her fast asleep.

Early Sunday morning, Samantha woke up to the sound of the phone buzzing on the dresser beside the bed. She quickly answered it, hoping it was Jonetta.

"Hello?"

"It's me, Sam. I'm at LAX. My plane just landed."

"I'm on my way, Sister. Give me about forty-five minutes; I'm on my way now. I mapped it out yesterday while I was sitting here bored to death. Do you know which gate?"

"I'm not sure. Look for the arriving flights on Delta Airlines Flight 103 when you come through the toll booth."

"Alright I'll see you in a few."

Samantha arrived at the entrance to Delta Airlines and slowed down looking for Gate 32. Within minutes, she spotted Jonetta coming out and tooted the horn.

"Hey, Sis!" Jonetta said, waving wildly!

"Hey, Girl. I'm sure glad to see a familiar face." Samantha responded warmly.

Jonetta opened the door and tossed her luggage in the back seat grabbing a towel out of her carry-on bag to wipe the sweat from her face.

"Damn! It's hot as hell out here!"

"Who are you telling? I been out here for almost a week and It's been like this since the day I arrived. Where's Trevon?"

"He should be in by 7 P.M tonight. He stayed behind to get confirmation of Cynthia's last known address from the private investigator."

"Damn, Sis. I could've been checking on that all this week instead of just sitting around here for free."

"Yeah. I'm sure any one of us could have located this place as popping as you claim it is, but he wants to handle everything himself. So let's let him take care of his business."

"His ass feeling guilty, that's all that is."

"You already know the deal so let him do him right now."

Later that evening, Trevon called Jonetta to let her know he had made it to Cali. She gave him the address and room number of the hotel. An hour and half later, there was a loud knock at the door. Samantha eased up to the peephole to see what asshole was knocking so hard while Jonetta jumped up with anticipation.

"It's that crazy-ass husband of yours beating on the door like he some damn law." Samantha blurted out and the beat of Jonetta's heart rate slowed to a normal pace. She pushed Samantha to the side with her hip and snatched the door open. Trevon walked in smiling from ear to ear, dragging his suitcase behind him.

"Hey! I thought we were supposed to pick you up at the airport?" Jonetta said.

"I went ahead and paid for a shuttle to bring me over here. I needed time to figure out our next move." Trevon replied.

"Did you get the address to the Chocolate Swirl?"

"The private investigator gave me every piece of information he had on the Chocolate Swirl and its operation. Only thing is, he has yet to get inside and actually see any of the girls."

"How the hell does he know if Cynthia was actually there? We may be on a wild goose chase."

"Let's ride up to the address and see who comes to the door. I can act as though I'm lost and see if he'll give a bitch some help." Sam responds.

The three got into the car and headed towards Hollywood Hills. Within the hour, Trevon veered left to the winding road, slowing to check the brick mail box for the address the P.I. provided him with.

"Here it is!" Trevon said proudly.

"This doesn't appear to be the type of neighborhood that someone would just break down in."

"I was thinking the same thing, Sam." Trevon replied.

"Let me out right here. I'll figure out what to say when I get to the door."

Jonetta got out of the car, rolled up both pants legs, and unbuttoned the first three buttons on her blouse. Taking a deep breath, she approached the door and rang the doorbell.

Boss got up off the couch and checked the monitor in his room before answering the door. "Hello, Sweet Lady! How can I help you?"

Jonetta was caught off guard by the mild-mannered young man. He didn't

Have any facial hair.

"My girl and I just came to town, and we are looking for somewhere to spread the love. We got your name from a girl by the name of Ingrid. She recommended we see you if we were trying to get money, Honey. She says you could show southern girls how to get some paper out this way and help a bitch get down about her hustle."

Boss took a step back, looked hard at Jonetta, and changed his demeanor instantly.

He blurted out, "Look, Lady. Whoever these people are that you made up in your head to come at me with, I have no knowledge of and furthermore, I don't know shit about what you're talking!"

Boss slammed the door in Jonetta's face and abruptly made his way to the King's Quarters to check the camera. He stood at the entrance to his suite, eyes fixed on the camera's shot of the street. He stalked Jonetta's every step back to the car. Paulette walked up and placed her arms around Boss.

"Is something wrong, Daddy?" Paulette's asked, seeing the puzzled look on his face.

"You know this bitch from somewhere?"

Paulette rounded the corner, and looked at the monitor, catching a glimpse of the woman from behind. She said nothing.

Jonetta quickly returned to the car and slid into the passenger seat. Trevon pulled off into the dusk dark of the evening with the lights off.

"I don't know if that was the right house. A young dude that couldn't have been any older than twenty-five or twenty-six years old answered the door. He had a fly twang to his voice, but he couldn't hold an ant for hostage."

"That was the right house, Trevon assured them. The P.I. told me to be on the lookout for a younger man with an intellectual-sounding voice. He may have forced Cynthia into the business here."

"Well that plan is fucked up! He seemed much smarter than to just let someone into his organization, especially at a moment's notice." Jonetta replied.

"How the hell was Cynthia lured in then?" Samantha demanded.

"Paulette may have been the bait for the young cat from the beginning and Cynthia, not knowing, was destined to be drawn in by the material things he may have offered her as soon as she touched down. Hell! If I didn't know any better, I would have been drawn in by the house alone!"

"Paulette knows both of us."

"We'll have to use that to our advantage." Jonetta said.

The trio made it back to the room and sat up until the wee hours of the morning, plotting a way to get inside Boss's doors. Samantha tried on several wigs and outfits to mask her voluptuous curves. She disappeared into the bathroom and came out a few minutes later with a blond wig thrown on top of her head and bright red lipstick accenting her lips.
"Damn, girl! You look like the whore on Carwash with your crazy ass!" Trevon yelled out.

"I'm trying to figure out a way to get in that damn house!" countered Sam.

"Oh, don't worry! I'll be up early in the morning looking for somebody back home that knows Paulette or her family. I know everybody in the Jets!" Jonetta said with confidence.

The next few days of their stay in California, were exhausting for the trio. They stayed cooped up in the hotel room and out of the public eye. By day, Jonetta searched through her phone book for anyone that may have had contact with Paulette in the last few months. Finally, on the third day her cell phone rang and it was Sasha.

"Hello? Aunt Jonetta, this is Sasha."

"Hey, Sasha. How's auntie's baby doing?"

"I'm fine. I was just calling to let you know I found Paulette's niece Crystal and she said she talks to her regular."

"How did you know I was even looking for Paulette?"

"I overheard Mama talking to Ingrid last night. So I asked Crystal did she ever hear from her aunt Paulette anymore. She said something about going to California last summer but her grandmother couldn't get the money for her flight."

"Who's her mother? Lakeisha or Cherry?"

"Neither. Her mother was the oldest. I think she told me her mother was killed in a car wreck when she was just a baby."

"Oh, that's right. Her mother was Carla, Joyce's oldest daughter. She was killed by a drunk driver when we were in the eighth grade and she was in her last year of high school. She was returning to class from having the baby and an old man's car jumped the curb at the bus stop. He hit her, killing her on impact. They ruled it an accident because he was an old white man with money. I remember that like it was yesterday. Paulette was so upset by the tragedy of her sister's death. She wouldn't come to school for at least a month, after they finally got up the money to bury her sister. Where is she living?"

"She's been living with her grandmother ever since I've known her."

"Sasha, you tell her to give me a call on my cell phone as soon as you see her."

"Will do and I love yawl. Tell Aunt Sam I said hello."

Sasha hung up the line and immediately headed out to the courtyard in search of her friend. She called her grandmother's house but there was no answer. Sasha found a seat on the bench close to the basketball court and watched as the athletes of the projects did their thing. She was in a zone watching the guys get selected by the different team captains for the next game. When her cell phone rang, she reached in her back pocket, retrieved her phone and checked the number.

"Hey girl, I called you earlier. Where you been?"

"I just came back from the mall with Big Mama. She bought me a few things for my trip to California, I'm leaving on Friday."

"Oh cool, so she was able to come up with the flight money this time?"

"Naw, my Aunt Paulette called and told me to tell Big Mama that she'd spring for my fare and I'll just have to work it off when I get there."

"When are you coming back?"

"I tried to ask her about that, but she hurried off the phone saying she had an important call coming in on the other line."

"Come out by the basketball court. I'm sitting on the bench watching Brandon and Myron."

"Ok. Let me put these clothes up and I'll be right out."

Crystal showed up and the two walked off. Sasha put in a call to Jonetta as instructed. The phone rang several times, and then it went to voicemail. Sasha pushed the recall button, but she was stopped by an incoming call.

"Here she is now." Sasha told her friend.

"Hello?" Crystal answered the phone.

"Sasha, did you call?"

"This is Crystal, Sasha's friend. She said you wanted to talk to me."

"Hey, Crystal. This is Jonetta. Have you heard from your Aunt Paulette lately?"

"Yes, ma'am. I'm supposed to be leaving for California on Friday to visit her."

"Oh, really? What time is she supposed to be picking you up from the airport?"

"I'm not sure, but all I know I'm getting' in Friday at LAX. My aunt Paulette has the itinerary since she's paying for everything."

"Listen real clearly, Crystal. I need you to get in touch with your aunt Paulette and ask her what time she is picking you up from the airport and call me back ASAP."

"Is everything alright, Mrs. Jonetta?"

"Yes, Baby. I was just down this way visiting family and wanted to take her out to dinner as a surprise while I am here."

"Wow! I'm sure she'll like that."

"It has to be a secret for it to be a surprise, though. Can you keep it a secret Crystal?"

"Yes, ma'am. I can definitely keep a secret. I'll get your number from Sasha and call you back as soon as I hear from her."

"Thanks, Crystal. And remember, it has to be a secret."

"I know, and I'll call you later."

"Bye."

The teenager handed the phone back to Sasha and walked off towards the basketball court.

"Okay. Aunt Jonetta, is there anything else?"

"No, and thanks so much Sasha for finding her for me."

"No problem. That's what family does for each other."

Jonetta was amazed at the way Sasha was handling herself. She knew the young woman held some of the same qualities as Ingrid, but she was fascinated with Sasha's words.

Days passed with no word from Crystal and Jonetta started to worry that the young girl had somehow let the secret slip and Paulette was now on to them. Out of the blue, her phone rang. Seeing it was Sasha's number, Jonetta exhaled.

"Hello?"

"Hey, Mrs. Jonetta. My granny's getting ready to drop me off at the airport. I didn't call you back earlier because my aunt just returned my call about an hour ago. She gave Big Mama my flight times. I should arrive at 8:15 California time according to what my granny wrote down."

"Great. I'll see you then."

Jonetta hung up the phone and alerted the others to get ready.

"What time is she getting in?" Trevon asked.

"She'll be at LAX in a couple of hours. We need to get a move on."

Samantha gathered her things as planned and the trio abruptly headed for the car. Trevon raced towards the highway and floored the pedal to the fast lane. Samantha slapped the blond wig on, smeared the red lipstick across her lips, and listened intently to Trevon's plan of action.

"If Paulette has company with her, I'll handle him. Just make sure we get the baby without making a scene."

"I got you, Bro."

Trevon pulled into the third story parking garage and went over the plan again. They spent the next hour going over the "what ifs and "just in cases. A few minutes before 8 P.M., Trevon pulled out of the parking garage and parked in the passenger pick up lane behind a set of yellow cabs. He went over the plan once more, making sure everyone was ready to move with precision.

Samantha exited the car and strolled back and forth up the walkway, stopping at times and posing as a passenger waiting to be picked up. She closely monitored every car that pulled to the curb in search of Paulette James. At exactly 8:41, she spotted a Black Range Rover with tinted windows pulling up to the curb of the fifteen-minute parking area. She watched as a woman got out of the passenger side and immediately recognized her middle school friend. She motioned for the others to get in position and made her way towards the ramp, trailing Paulette's every step.

Eight minutes later, Paulette came through the doors with her arm around her niece's shoulder. Sam dropped her cigarette and closely trailed behind the two. Moving faster, she closed the gap and motioned for Trevon to make his move. He started the car and tried to pull out, but he was blocked by a cab. Samantha sprang into action and grabbed the young girl by the arm.

Seeing the commotion, Paulette reached into her left pocket to retrieve the stun gun, but Sam beat her to the punch. She doused Paulette with pepper spray and punched her twice in the face, causing the dazed woman to release the grip she had on the young girl and the stun gun. Crystal screamed out for help.

Jonetta got out the car and was confronted by Boss. He backhanded her with his left hand, halting her forward motion. He then grabbed the frightened teenager and rushed her over to the Range Rover. Samantha yelled for Crystal to get out of the truck, but the shock of it all was too much for the young girl to process. She panicked as Boss rounded the truck and jumped in.

Jonetta quickly recovered and tried to open the passenger door to get Crystal, but leaving his bottom bitch behind to fend for herself, Boss pulled into traffic, barely missing an oncoming shuttle. Trevon finally got the rental car out of the jam and pulled up to the scene. Jonetta stumbled back to where Samantha was holding Paulette hostage, grabbed her around the neck, and the two forced the woman into the back seat of the rental as Trevon sped off. Samantha reached into Paulette's pockets to see what she had been trying so desperately to reach, and she stumbled upon the 1000-volt stun gun.

Trevon looked on with revenge in his heart as Jonetta wiped the blood from her mouth.

"This is what the bitch was reaching for!" Samantha exclaimed. Sam flipped the switch on the gadget and hit Paulette with a strong dose at full voltage.

Fifteen minutes later, Paulette awoke and stared at her captors intensely. Sam removed the wig off her head and she spoke directly at Paulette.

"Where's Cynthia's baby? What lie did you use to manipulate her to come to the west coast, knowing she would be playing hardball?"

"I didn't ask her to come here. She came on her own! What the hell are ya 'll doing here?" Paulette yelled with aggravation.

"Did your niece come here on her on too? Did you pay for Cynthia's flight?"

"I told you, Cynthia came here on her on."
Samantha pushed the stun gun into her side and demanded through clinched teeth. "Where's Devianna, Paulette?"

"I don't know. Why in the hell do you keep on asking me about some baby? What baby are you talking about?"

"Cynthia's baby, Bitch! Don't play games with me!" Jonetta jumped in.
Samantha moved over to clear any contact with Paulette and hit her again with the stun gun, this time knocking her completely unconscious.

"Go to sleep, Bitch. I m tired of hearing your bullshit ass lies."

"Let's get her back to the room and see what information she can give us to get inside the house." Trevon reasoned.

"We need to hurry. That little girl's life could be hanging in the balance." Samantha added.

"Let's call the police and tell them there's been a kidnapping and give them the address of the house. "Jonetta offered.

"That's definitely a no go. The private investigator says he's 100% sure the police are somehow in with the operation of the Chocolate Swirl."

"Well, let's see if the pimp will go for a trade. Fair exchange ain't no robbery." Samantha suggested with a laugh.

Trevon drove the seventy-six miles back to the hotel with caution, making sure not to attract attention from the police by speeding. He wanted to get Paulette back to the room safely so he could obtain the information he need to locate the baby's whereabouts.

Boss makes it to the mansion in record time. He pulled the truck into his garage and quickly closed it behind him. He looked over at the frightened teen and tried to assure her that things weren't as they appeared, but the look of sheer terror on her face signaled her fear of him.

"Get out the car." Boss demanded.

Crystal nervously fingered the latch and bumped her shoulder against the door to exit, only to find that the passenger's door was locked. The latch slipped from her grip and she hit the side of the door with full force. Boss snapped at the sound of someone slamming his precious car door. He grabbed the unsuspecting girl by the neck and started choking her. Her screams were muffled as she desperately tried to fight off her attacker. She kicked and punched at Boss with a barrage of blows from all angles. He finally subdued his victim with a solid punch to the temple, knocking the teen unconscious. He got out of the car, crept to the garage door, and put his ear to the metal to see if anyone was following him before unloading the young woman's limp body from the truck.

Trevon pulled into the parking lot of the hotel and dropped off Jonetta with instructions to open the back entrance to the pool area. "Make sure no one's lurking in the hallway when I pull up." He added.

Jonetta waved her hand to acknowledge his request as she ran her fingers through her hair and adjusted her clothes. She strolled towards the entrance of the hotel, eased past the desk with her head down, and preceded to their room. She unlocked the door and left it propped open. She slowly moved down the hallway until she was sure their safety wouldn't be jeopardized.

Meanwhile, Trevon impatiently sat in the cut with the lights off and the motor running. He tried to cover his nervousness but he was wondering what was taking her so long.

"She needs to bring her ass on."

"Calm down, Bro. This bitch ain't going anywhere! If she wakes up, I'll hit her with a double dose."

"Be careful not to kill her, though. We need her right now."

Jonetta reached the back door of the hotel, covered the light, and waved for the others to come on. Trevon pulled up to the gate, jumped out of the driver's seat, and the two dragged Paulette's body unseen into the building. Trevon returned to the car and removed the plates in case they were made in the commotion at the airport. He re-entered the room and saw that Paulette was coming around. Immediately, Trevon began a round of interrogation, but after dealing with Boss for so long, Paulette took Trevon's aggressive behavior as a joke.

"Look here, bitch! The only chance you have of surviving is to tell us where the baby is!"

"I don't know shit about any baby and if I did, I wouldn't tell you mutha fucka's! Do what you gon' do! If anything happens to me you'll wish you never set foot in Cali. Boss is comin' after me!"

"I have something special for your ass." Trevon calmly strolled over to his luggage and located the pliers he brought with him. He quickly moved back to the bed to face his victim and slipped a pillow case over her head.

"Sam, cut this bitch's vocal chords off if she makes a sound! Babe, come hold her legs."

Jonetta moved towards the bed to do as Trevon instructed. She wrapped her hands around Paulette's legs and held them in place while Trevon snatched her pinky toe nail clean off the skin.

Paulette squirmed, but not a sound escaped her.

"Where's the baby?" Trevon demanded.

"Fuck you and these bitches! I'll never tell you shit about my daddy."

Samantha punched Paulette in the face with a hammer fist and immediately blood spurted from the top of her brow.

"Boss will never let you mutha fucka's get away with putting your paws on Me.! Y'all have fucked with the wrong bitch for real! I can assure you he's in the area looking for you mutha fuckas with a squad of killers with him."

"We don't care about Boss or whoever this punk is supposed to be! We came for the Cynthia's baby!"

"I don't know shit about Cynthia or her little girl."

"Then how did you know it was a little girl, you lying ass hoe?" Trevon lunges at Paulette's throat with both hands. He connected with her jugular vein and her eyes began to protrude from their sockets. After a few seconds, he released his grip to allow Paulette a gasp of air. Then, he vice gripped her neck for the second round while Jonetta looked on in sheer terror that they'd face another murder case. Trevon once again released his hold on Paulette and he saw tears rolling down her face. He pulled out his cell phone and shoved it in Paulette's grill.

"Here! Dial the number!"

Paulette just stared at Trevon with hostile eyes. "Go ahead and kill me! I ain't giving up shit!

"Dial the fuckin' number before your wish is granted."

Paulette took the phone and reluctantly she dialed the number to the mansion. The phone rang several times and then it went straight to voicemail.

"I told you he was out looking for yawl."

"Listen, Paulette. No man that'll leave a woman stuck out like he did you tonight has your best interest at heart."

Paulette softened a little at the thought of Boss caring about her. "Boss truly adores all of his women. I'm his bottom bitch right now and proud of it. I am the Queen Bee and I run that house."

"Paulette, will you get off the bullshit? Pimps don't give a damn about a bitch if she ain't bringing in the cash flow." Samantha snarled.

"No, Sam. Boss loves me and he takes care of me. . He's made that clear a thousand times."

"That's to get it in your head so that you start to believe it. It's all game, Paulette! I thought you were smarter than that."

"He's the only man that ever made me feel loved." Paulette continued, suddenly afraid that Sam might be right. "With Boss I have security. He protects me and I do it all for him. We live the good life in a fine ass mansion. And I get paid!"

"It's a false sense, Paulette. It's hope that can never be cashed in."

Paulette was clearly confused. She sat up on her elbows with her head leaning against the headboard. She had never heard anyone speak against Boss or the way he handled his business. Deep in her heart, she felt there was truth in what Sam was saying, but Boss's words still held the strongest impact on her beliefs. Paulette was terrified of what Boss would do if he ever got wind that she spoke against him. Samantha had said her piece and was at the end of her rope with Paulette.

"Listen," Sam interrupted. "Get him on the phone and tell him that we're willing to make a deal with him. For the safe return of Devianna and Crystal, he can have your stupid ass back."

"Wait a minute; Sam let me get my thoughts together." Paulette pleaded as she sat stoically second-guessing the facade she'd been living behind. The fact that she hadn't seen her family in the last five years angered her even more. She asked for a towel to wipe her face and stared at Samantha, closely guarding her every movement. Sweat escaped her pours and her nostrils flared when she recalled Boss's episode with Mrs. Annie after discovering she'd betrayed Boss by helping Cynthia get away.

"I promise you that baby is not in the house anymore. When Cynthia escaped, she took the baby with her. I assumed that she and the child had returned to Texas."

"Paulette, Cynthia's dead. She killed herself a few weeks ago. That's why we're here, trying to find out where the baby is."

"She's dead?" Paulette asked, self-doubt creeping into her voice.

"We buried Cynthia a little over a week ago now," a dry- eyed Samantha said.

Paulette started to feel the heat of being responsible for Cynthia's death. She knew her intentions for the young woman were selfish. She just wanted to please Boss. She had exposed Cynthia's vulnerability to her pimp, assuring him that she'd get the naive woman there by any means necessary. With the lure of her third unsuspecting victim, Paulette was moved to "bottom bitch" and relinquished of her own financial responsibilities. The hours away from Boss and his influence had given Paulette time to think rationally. The guilt began to take over as she realized how many lives she had put in harm's way. Tears welled up in her eyes as Paulette curled up in a fetal position. The hardness of her heart softened and she cried out, begging for forgiveness.

"I'm so sorry, Cynthia! I didn't mean to hurt you. I brought you into that house knowing my lifestyle would destroy you! I thought you'd get used to it and be okay. I wish I could trade my life for yours, but it's too late!"

"You can make up for it by helping us find the baby." Trevon intruded, taking advantage of Paulette's weakened state.

"Okay, Trevon, I'll do it. I can do much more than help you find the baby. I want to stop Boss's madness before someone else ends up dead inside the 'Swirl."

Trevon had no idea what Paulette's comment meant. He wondered if their childhood friend was now truly down for the cause. He wasn't at all convinced that her loyalty had suddenly changed. But he listened to her tell her story. The four sat up the remainder of the night while Paulette went over every aspect of Boss's operation that she had access to. She confirmed what the PI had reported, that most of the clients were either high-priced or hidden behind the badge. Strangely, she sat with a menacing grin on her face as if she enjoyed describing the heinous events that she'd witnessed since she was lured to Boss years earlier.

"Let's follow the plan and see how it works out."

Early the next morning, Paulette called the mansion and the call was quickly transferred to Boss.

"What bitch is this?" Boss demanded when he answered.

"Daddy, come and get me, I escaped last night and hid in the garbage dumpster till this morning. I need for you to pick me up." Boss sat in the lounge area with Crystal locked in his arms.

"Look whore, you've been away from my influence for more than twelve hours! You expect me to believe you were in some dumpster hiding all night?"

Trevon was no longer able to contain himself. He grabbed the phone out of Paulette's hand and charged into Boss with full force.

"Look, Nigga! Cut through the small talk and get down to business! We have your bottom bitch! Are you willing to make a deal or not?"

"A deal for what? You got a bitch on her last leg you're trying to trade off for this young, vibrant, tasty little thing that I have in my custody! Who in the hell trades a Bentley for a hooptie, fool? I tell you what. You keep the bitch and get whatever years in the game she got left in her, and I'll raise this newbie like a real daddy should do his baby girl." With that, he ended the call.

Paulette was stunned at the words she heard from Boss's mouth. Here he was, the man who promised her she was irreplaceable, and that he'd love her forever.

He had just talked about her as if she was garbage. She sat on the edge of the bed, her heart swimming in a sea of emotions. She was filled with regret for the years she had abandoned her family for the man that cared nothing about her safe return. He didn't care what happened to her at all. She was further reminded when Samantha began her "I told you so's".

"Snap out of it, Paulette! Quit acting like a fucking stew-head! I told your dumb ass, a nigga like that stops giving a damn about a bitch the moment she stops bringing in his bread."

"That's enough, Sam. We need to move fast and do what we need to do to get Crystal out of there," Jonetta interrupted.

"What's the plan, then?" Sam asked.

"Trevon has to be the one to get us inside."

"What?" he asked confused about the change of plans. "What do you think I can do that we haven't thought of already?

"If you really want to find the baby and save Crystal, force your way in by any means necessary like the warrior you are."

Chapter 9

Boss forcefully escorted the terrified teen tightly noosed in a diamond bedazzled dog leash. He looked at his newest project and smiled, contemplating the years of service he was looking forward to getting out of the young firm body standing before him.

"Listen here, pretty lady. You follow my rules and I promise to make sure your every need is met."

Crystal nodded to acknowledge her obedience with the man's sick request. Crystal was accustomed to dealing with the atrocities of life from the environment she was raised in. But under the layer of what appeared to be the most promising catch for Boss to date, was a gritty, vivacious kid from the Como Projects determined not to become a statistic in the prostitution game. Growing up under her grandparents' guidance, she was always taught to protect herself at all times. At an early age, her grandfather taught her several aggressive military-style combat moves to free herself from harm's way.

Boss jerked on the neck chain and pulled the young girl in the direction of the basement. Crystal stumbled, steps behind her captor's every movement. Several women passed by, seemingly unfazed by the dog leash strapped around her neck. When they reached the basement, Crystal smelled the stench of a decayed body filling her nostrils. Boss cuffed her to the torture chamber and slid a bowl of water towards her feet and a plate with two slices of stale bread.

"Here this is your dinner for the next few days. Eat slowly," Boss directed and turned to walk away.

"But you don't have to do this to me, Daddy. Whatever it is you need me to do to prove my loyalty, I'll do it," Crystal pleaded. But Boss was in no mood for negotiations.

"Look, bitch. This is only preparation for the next step in life. It's the 'You prove me wrong, you get what you need' stage."

"I don't need this shit and I ain't gonna eat out of no damn bowl either, so take this with you." The young hostage became enraged with the demands of her captor. She kicked the bowl and plate from under her and out of reach.

"You're going to regret that." Boss replied, and left her alone in her misery.

Her hunger got the best of her by the end of the second day. Crystal's body started to wither as she sat chained to a corner of the basement, unable to reach either the bowl of water or the bread. On the third day of being held in captivity, Boss entered the basement and was thrown for a loop. Crystal huddled in the corner, clinging to life, but on the brink of death, it seemed. Boss felt a twinge of remorse but decided she had brought it on herself. Nevertheless, in a moment of compassion, he freed his young hostage. He walked Crystal up to the kitchen and told his new bottom bitch to get her something to eat. Relieved, Crystal thanked him and slumped into a chair waiting for nourishment. Anything would do.

As the days slid slowly by, the chances of finding baby Devianna were getting slimmer by the hour. The stress of not knowing whether the child was dead or alive, weighed heavy on Trevon's mind. It was hard enough with two women in the hotel room. Now he had to deal with Paulette, too, and he still didn't trust her.

He sat staring out the window in a daze until his attention was diverted to a vision forming in the clouds. He leaned against the window, eyes affixed on the motionless clouds, when suddenly out of nowhere; he spotted what appeared to be the outline of his twin brother lingering in one of the clouds. Physically shaken by the sighting of Devon, Trevon stepped away from the window and rubbed both eyes in total disbelief. With tears at the brink of his eyes, he looked around and caught Jonetta staring at him.

"Trevon, are you okay?" She asked, seeing her husband upset.

"I'm go-g-g good." Trevon stuttered in response.

"Babe, calm down before you over exert yourself again."

Jonetta walked over to Trevon, still by the window, and wrapped her arms around him.

"I said I'm okay," he argued, pulling back.

He leaned towards the window to see if the cloud was still there and again, Trevon saw the image of his brother.

"The baby is safe. Dude is soft. Get the young girl and go home now."

Did Trevon imagine hearing his brother's voice? He pulled away from Jonetta and turned to face the window again, awaiting the next message. But the clouds slowly dissipated into thin air.

"We have to get a move on if we're going to get the baby out of harm's way." Trevon said, not willing to Miss Devon's wakeup call a second time.

With Trevon at the wheel, the four of them pulled on to the access road and into the building traffic. It took fifty-one minutes to arrive at the beginning of the long winding road that led to Chocolate Swirl.

"Make a left right here and just follow the winding road. The house is up here on the right." Paulette said. They already knew because they had been there before.

When they reached the mansion, Trevon eased off the pedal, allowing the car to roll freely. Paulette pointed at the well-secured mansion and the four discussed the most logical way to get inside. After deciding there was no other way to breech the residence other than to kick in the front door, Trevon pulled off and called his cousin.

Carson answered on the second ring.

"Hey, Cuz! What's going on out there?" Carson asked, relieved to hear from Trevon.

Trevon began to rattle off a series of unfamiliar words and phrases in code, leaving everyone other than Samantha completely dumbfounded. Sam smiled mysteriously, as she listened to Trevon roll the Nig Latin phrases quickly off his tongue. Sam was fully aware from the conversation that they were about to get into some real gangster shit. Trevon ended the call and checked his surroundings, catching Sam's big grin in his rearview mirror.

"What's up Sam?" he sighed.

"Shizit Jizust rizeady tizu hizandle thizat lilo bizness, gizet bizabee sizista frezeed and blizo thizis mizark izas izoff tha mizap. Sam fired off with precision. ("Shit! Just ready to handle this little business, gets baby sister freed, and blaze this mark ass off the map!")

Trevon looked over his shoulder, amazed that Sam not only knew the talk, but was quite fluent with it.

Carson arrived, fatigued from his long drive, the burners tightly tucked in his luggage. The plan was set in motion. Trevon was careful not to disclose too much of the plot in the company of Paulette. He was not at all convinced of her sincerity.

"Damn! I'm sure glad you didn't get jammed at the airport with the heat."

"That's why I brought the plastic pieces instead of the 45 caliber you ask for. "Carson replied.

"Yeah, but you didn't wrap these mutha fucker's up good at all."

"They were wrapped good enough to get through the check points. That's all that matters."

"Yeah. Well we gonna handle our business and give this nigga a dose of some act right!"

"That's exactly what I came for!"

Trevon throws his arm over Carson's shoulder and the two walked towards the hotel room.

Hours later under the darkness of night, the five headed for the target destination. Trevon and Carson were in front, strapped and mentally prepared for confrontation. Jonetta trailed behind with Samantha guarding Paulette as she nervously chewed on her nails. As Jonetta pulled on to the street and shut off her lights, Paulette barraged her with questions, seeming more concerned about Boss's well-being, than that of her own flesh and blood. Sam grew irate as Paulette squirmed in the seat next to her.

"Paulette, don't get all antsy and stupid on me right now." Sam said, sensing a change of heart in Paulette the closer they got to the residence.

"I'm sorry. I just don't want anything to happen to Boss." Paulette responded.

"Look, I don't know what you're going through, Paulette, but you really need to chill and stick to the plan."

Jonetta eased around and approached the house with caution. When she bumped the breaks twice to get a better look at the cars parked in the driveway, Paulette seized the moment, leaping from the vehicle and tumbling to the pavement. Jonetta slammed on the breaks, throwing the car into park as Sam jumped out in hot pursuit. But Paulette loomed a few steps ahead of her, making it to the door and beating on it with both hands as she screamed at the top of her lungs.

"Boss! Boss! Let me in! They're trying to kill us."

Seconds later, Sam made it to the porch and collided, body-on into her childhood friend. She grabbed Paulette by the shoulders and slammed her to the concrete, immediately halting her screams. When Trevon looked up and saw the car door open, he knew instantly that something had gone wrong. He pulled up to the scene and slammed on the breaks, causing treads of rubber marks in the street. Trevon slid the mask over his face and rushed out of his car with the gun in his right hand and Carson on his bumper. Realizing Paulette's antics may have caused the plot to be foiled, Trevon raced to the door and threw himself into it, but the thick wooden door wouldn't budge. Boss was relaxing in the lounge when he heard the sound of a battering ram at his front door. He hurried out of the lounge past the front door to his suite, slamming the door behind him. When he looked up at the monitor, he was shocked by the hooded men with pistols in tow, attempting to gain entry to his palace. Shaken to the core, he disappeared into the closet and scrambled to get the safe open, allowing Trevon and Carson ample opportunity to get into the mansion. The door broke on the third attempt and the mayhem kicked into high gear. Screams of terror escaped the mouths of the women scrambling for safety as Trevon and Carson entered with guns drawn. Carson grabbed one of the girls, placing a pistol to her head. Petrified, she whimpered at the feeling of cold steel pressed against her temple.

"Shut up, bitch! And lead me to your punk ass daddy."

"I swear I don't know anything! The woman pleaded, her arms

flailing wildly.

"Either you have a sudden memory spurt, or I blow your mutha fucking head off!" Carson threatened.

Trevon rounded the corner and peeped into the empty hallway, then back at Carson who was waving his gun, signaling the room closest to him and the camera above the door. Trevon leaned against the wall to pass the eye in the sky and bashed the lens out with the butt of his gun.

"You release the girl willingly or I kick the door in and end your life! It makes no difference to me! You make the call, bitch!" Trevon shouted, but there was no response.

Boss was distraught with anxiety, unable to remember the combination to the safe.

After a few tense seconds, Trevon backed up, booted the door from its hinges, and moved within a few feet of the devil himself. Kneeling over the closed safe, Boss's heart fluttered as he realized he would have to defend himself alone. The cowardly woman-beater abruptly changed his demeanor as he stared down the barrel of the pistol.

"Listen, man, we can make a deal for the girl." Boss pleaded.

"I don't make deals with punks who kidnap children and beat up women!" Trevon maneuvered through the room like a professional hit man. When he reached the entrance to the closet, he stared at Boss with authority and blurted out, "You're a dead man."

"Man, please don't kill me. I'll do anything you want me to do. I'll play whatever position you want me to play, bro, just don't pull the trigger! Please, man! Please!" Boss was lullabying to the choir.

"Let me see how well you play dead, mutha fucka!" Trevon muttered as he fired three shots into Boss's face, peeling the top of his hairline back exposing the white of his flesh."

Carson pushed the girl into the room and she stopped in her tracks, breathless at the sight of brain matter and hair splattered inside the closet. The gruesomeness of the crime was overbearing. She collapsed to her knees, vomiting on the carpet.

"Come on, man, let's get the girl and get the hell up out of here!" Carson urged.

"Pick her up and bring her on!"

Carson grabbed the half-dressed captive by the back of her neck and dragged her over to get a first-hand account of the bullet-riddled body. She shook nervously, eyes fixed on the lifeless man she once called Boss.

"Tell me where Crystal is before you end up with your head exploded like this mutha fucka here!" Trevon spoke through clinched teeth.

Convinced of the danger she now faced, she cracked and her mouth ran like diarrhea. "Last I heard she was locked in the Queen's Quarters. It's down the hall in the southern wing."

"Are you sure?"

"Y- y-yes, she stammered."

"Are you sure enough to bet your life on it?"

"I mean, all I heard is one of the girls saying she heard screams coming from the room and that she thought Boss was breaking the new girl in. I don't know for sure."

"Cool, I appreciate your honesty." Trevon nodded at the woman. "Let's go, man.

"Just a minute, Cuz. I got some business to handle," he replied. Carson lowered the automatic to the skull of the frightened girl and dropped two into her cranium, parting the back of her head open. He wanted to be sure there were no living witnesses to identify them and send them back to prison.

Then he walked out in search of the Queen's Quarters.

Trevon rambled through the dead man's suite until he located the video's main frame hidden behind an expensive Picasso painting. He snatched the entire unit from the cubby hole, leaving power cords dangling from their fixtures. Next, he headed to the front of the house to check on Jonetta and Sam. Trevon smiled as he saw them loading Paulette's limp body into the trunk of the rental car. He motioned for them to come back in to search the house for Crystal and the baby.

Carson, Trevon and Jonetta swiftly cleared the first two rooms opening doors as Sam stood watch by the front. When they found more girls and terrified tricks with their pants down, they slammed the doors behind them. In the third room, Trevon recognized one of the johns as the private eye he had been paying to find Cynthia.

This was the man who claimed he couldn't get in to the Swirl.

"So is this what I was paying you for?" Trevon demanded.

"Uh, uh, uh…look, man, it took me a while to get in here."

"Well, it looks like you all the way in. And the girl I told you to find is missing.

"Carson walked up to Trevon asking, "Is this the punk you were payin' cuz?"

"Yeah, man."

"Then he's got to go."

"Do it. Handle yo' business."

"Say no more." he responded, as he shot the P.I. in the chest, knocking him against the wall.

It wasn't long before Trevon heard the sound of banging coming from the last room on the left.

He dashed to the closed door demanding, "Crystal, is that you in there?"

"Somebody help me please!"

"Crystal?"

"Yes, it's me! Please help me!" The teenager shouted through the door.

"Stand back away from the door." Trevon yelled out as he kicked the door in. Upon entry, he found the young woman standing naked, welts covering ninety per cent of her body. Outraged, he approached the frantic Crystal and slid the mask just above his eyebrows so she could see him.

The teenager was relieved to see a familiar face. She extended her arms out to embrace Trevon and he cautioned her to stop. Skeptical of the camera catching a glimpse of his tattoos, he grabbed the sheet from the bed and beckoned for Crystal.

"Here put this on and get on my back. I'll get us out of here.

Crystal wrapped herself in the sheet and climbed on his back. They exited the room, gun stretched out in military style. He made it to the front of the house, where the others, was waiting.

"Come on, Cuz. Let's roll."

The five left the mansion as the sound of police sirens loomed closer by the second. Trevon placed Crystal into the backseat, closed the door and got in front. Jonetta pulled off first, leading the way back down the winding road with Trevon and Carson close behind. She made it down the hill and turned on to the main street, trunk knocking like a 1000-watt amplifier. Her heart raced to overdrive as she passed the first mob of squad cars. One shined his bright flashlight into the car, causing the hair on the back of Jonetta's neck to stand at attention.

"Damn! Are they onto us?"

"Stay low. They're passing," Sam replied, trying to stay as calm as possible. She knew that if they were stopped, it would be an automatic life sentence if not the death penalty. Jonetta eased onto the freeway and blended into the light flow of traffic, exhaling the gasp of air she was holding in.

They made it back to the hotel and Crystal was kept in the car until Paulette was brought into the room, stun gun pressed into her spine. Jonetta hurried out and notified Samantha to hold tight. She was getting another room to hold the trash in her trunk.

In the days following the murders, Trevon nervously paced the floor of the hotel room waiting for the mansion murders to be the top story on the news. He
Was relieved after the first couple of days passed and the heinous acts didn't get any attention. On the third day, he began the process of cleanup. He dismantled the murder weapons and instructed Carson to dispose of them along the highway, miles apart.

With the weight of the world on his shoulders, Trevon struggled with the possibility of having to kill Paulette. She had played the others with an intriguing story, claiming she was traumatized by her captor. But he wasn't the least bit moved by her performance. He strolled into the adjoining room where the friend-turn-traitor was being held, and went right into his "Nig Latin" spill with Carson.

"Wizah yizu thizank weze shizould dizu wizith thizis breezy?
(What you think we should do with this broad?)

"Mizan weze alrizeady hizave tizu bizodies izon izour hizands,

Weze sizurely dizont nizeed iziiny mizore hizeat." (Man, we already have two bodies on our hands! We surely don't need any more heat.)

"Bizut wize agrizeed frizcm thiza begizznig thizat wize wizouldnt lizeve iziny izof thiza izinimys wizitness Bezehizind" (But we agreed from the beginning that we wouldn't leave any of the enemy's witnesses behind.)

"Wizel tizake iza vizote izan cizee izf shizee lzives izor dizies" (We'll take a vote and see if she should live or die.)

The vote was tallied up among the four and Paulette was unanimously sentenced to die by lethal injection. Even though she'd been a childhood friend, they could not forgive her for sacrificing both Cynthia and Crystal to the evil whims of Boss. Though she had pretended to help them save Crystal and the baby, she had turned and warned Boss trying to save her own hide. They could have all easily been killed by him had they not dealt with him so quickly without mercy.

Later that evening, Sam set the plan in motion. She jumped into the car and rode through the 'hood until she found what appeared to be the " hoe stroll." She parked and blended right in with the flow of women getting their hustle on by walking the boulevard. One woman slowed her pace to flag a potential client down, and Sam made her move. She eased alongside the hooker and stared down at her arm looking for the track marks usually left by the needles.

"Excuse me, Miss Lady, but this car coming is a regular John of mines, and I'd appreciate it if you would back up off of me!"

"Look. I ain't trying to steal your clients. I'm just down here to get a gram of that black tar heroin and get back to the house."

"Who are you down here representin'?"

"Bitch, I represent Boss from the Hollywood Hills and he doesn't like a bitch answering a lot of questions, so make that your last one!"

"Oh really? Everybody wants to work for Boss! He gets a bitch paid with them high-end clients."

"I really don't have the time or the patience for small talk. I have to get back to the mansion and get to work."
"I'm sure."
The prostitute slid her hand into the shifted wig plopped down on her head and pulled out two small baggies. Sam examined the product, and then made her purchase. She turned and strolled off towards the car.
She quickly pulled away from the curb and spotted a junkie leaned against the wall shooting up. She bumped her breaks and from the passenger-side window, and offered the man a twenty-dollar bill for the bloody rig he was using. Happy to know where his next fix would come from, he quickly pulled the needle from his arm, wrapped it in tissue, and removed the dirty T-shirt he was wearing. He approached the vehicle and tossed the rig on the backseat as instructed. He reached through the window, grabbed the crispy bill, and rushed back into the cover of darkness.

Samantha returned to the hotel and entered the room where Carson and Trevon impatiently kept watch over a praying Paulette. When Sam entered the room, Carson aimed his gun.
"Hey! It's me! Sam!
"Yizu tizake kizare iziof yizor bizinezess?" Trevon asked. (You take care of your business?)
Sam pulled the newspaper from her jacket and unrolled the dingy T-shirt on the bed.
"Wizat thiza hizel iz thiziz?" (What the hell is this?)
With the end of a newspaper, Sam spread the musty shirt open and revealed the blood drawn up in the cylinder of the dirty needle. Trevon nodded his approval and gave her two thumbs up. He disappeared into the bathroom. Returning in just a few minutes, he had filled the needle with the hazardous substance from the baggies and neatly wrapped it in the two white face cloths.
"Here. Take care of your business," Trevon said as he handed the towels to Samantha.
Hearing the boldness in his voice, Paulette sensed the danger headed in her direction. She lifted her head up momentarily to see Samantha's right hand drawn back in attack mode. Tears streamed from her face as the fear consumed her.
Paulette goes into a frenzy. "No!" She screamed. "Don't do it!

You can't kill me! We like family!"

"No, "Sam said calmly. "We stopped being family the day you lured Cynthia and her baby here to do your dirty work. You stopped being family when you turned your own sister's child out to your pimp. You don't know the meaning of family, Paulette."

By then, Paulette was crying and begging. "Please don't let them kill me, Lord! Have mercy!"

These were the last words she spoke. Samantha plunged the syringe into her neck and thumbed all 90cc's of smack directly into her bloodstream. Paulette's eyes rolled to the back of her head and her body convulsed until it seemed to flat line.

Trevon wrapped the body up in a blanket and waited until the dark of night to move. At midnight, Carson pulled off into a rural area and the two discarded the body into the tall brush. They wiped their hands clean of the last witness. But Paulette's prayers to the Savior wouldn't go unheard.

Chapter 10

Unable to sleep from envisioning the murdered victims in his nightly dreams, Trevon slumped over in the loveseat of his second floor media room, tightly clutching the empty shot glass in his hand. He had long since distanced himself from the attempt on his father's life, writing it off as good sense, but the murders of Paulette and the female witness at the Chocolate Swirl were eating at his soul like a hungry vulture. He staggered over to the bar, poured himself a second double shot of Jim Beam, and slammed it down his throat in an attempt to find some solace. Leaning against the bar to keep from falling, he spotted the butt of a snub-nosed 38 peeking out the cabinet. He stared at the handle, contemplating suicide as a way to end his misery. The loss of his mother at the age of fifteen, his brother mistakenly murdered on his behalf, and the killer turning out to be his very own father were all driving him to the boiling point. Deciding on a game of Russian roulette to solve his problems, he rounded the bar to retrieve the revolver and loaded a single bullet into the cylinder. He spun the chamber twice and placed the gun to his temple. With his mother's words of encouragement pounding in the back of his subconscious, he put the fate of his existence into her and God's hands.

"If I'm supposed to live, Lord, it's all up to you. I know I've been a bad man and if it's my time to go, I'm ready to leave here tonight. Trevon closed his eyes and squeezed the trigger, but the sound of two metals colliding together snapped him back to reality. God had spared his life. The Teflon bullet sat one slot beyond reach of the firing pin. Shaken to the core, Trevon dropped the pistol on the counter and fell to the floor in tears. The drunken man longed for answers as to why the Lord had left him behind to face the music without his twin. The questions clouded his mind until he drifted off into a deep sleep.

Early the next morning, he woke up to find the media room in shambles. Several shot glasses were strewn about the carpet, and the empty whiskey bottle sat upright next to the loveseat. He braced himself to stand, but the effects of Jim Beam pounded in his head like a heavy weight prize fighter. His arms gave way and he fell back on the carpet. Trevon was in serious need of counseling to erase the temptation of last evening, but he was afraid to tell anyone of his plan to take his own life. For months, he had been struggling with the feeling of being less than worthy, while putting up a facade that everything was fine. All he knew was he needed something to restore some peace within.

Crystal underwent a series of operations to heal the deep lashes inflicted on her young body. Physically tormented, she required bandages and gauze for weeks. Emotionally drained, she remained withdrawn from everyone throughout her stay in the hospital. After being released from Baylor Medical Center, she became a permanent fixture in the Barnes home while she prepared to start a new life as a junior at the ritzy high school near their house.
 By the time the first quarter of the semester ended, Crystal had excelled as an honor student. By her senior year, the once-precocious teen ranked third in her class and was voted most likely to succeed. But trouble lurked in the cut and her past would soon hunt her down like a thief in the night.

After a few months of living in the Barnes home, Crystal started to notice a change in Trevon's demeanor, and it worsened by the week. Awakened many nights by the sound of his voice screaming out the names "Devianna" and "Li'l Sam," Crystal could see that he was an emotional wreck. She tried talking to him on several occasions, but to no avail. He kept his distance regarding her. Feeling rejected, and with no other father figure available, Crystal started to rebel.

Jonetta bumped the curb at the high school and hit the lock on the driver's door of the BMW, signaling Crystal to get out the car.

"Have a productive day, Crystal."

"I will, Mama. Thanks for dropping me off early."

Crystal sprang from the car, waved goodbye and trotted off in the direction of the cafeteria.

As Jonetta released the brake, she watched her daughter's movements in the rearview mirror. She quickly made a U-turn back into the drop off area when she saw Crystal suddenly change direction and dash off to the left. Jonetta parked and followed her trail to see what she was up to. Crystal rounded the building and ran into a mob of kids headed in all directions. When the concerned mother followed the bright yellow Sponge Bob back pack making a right turn into a class room, she breathed a sigh of relief. Jonetta continued her journey, pausing outside the closed classroom door. She peeped inside the small frame window and saw that the classroom was empty. When she turned the doorknob and entered the room, she was shocked to find Crystal hugging an older man. Of course, she snapped.

"What the fuck!"

Crystal cut her off and hurriedly tried to explain. "It's not what you think, Mom. Mr. Robertson has been helping me keep my grades up and I was just thanking him."

Fuming, Jonetta demanded, "Crystal! What the hell is going on here?"

"Just like I said! I was just showing my teacher a little appreciation for helping me out!" She fired off rebelliously.

"First of all, who in the hell do you think you're you talking to?"

"Ma'am, I can ......"

"No!" Jonetta snapped with her palm aimed at his face. "You just shut your mouth and I'll deal with your ass in a minute."

"But, Mom! Nothing happened!"

"But Mom my ass! I know the difference between a friendly hug and lust!

Jonetta turned back to the teacher and yelled, "And what the hell you call yourself doing, comforting young girls until you can get them to bed?"

The Boss Take Over

"Ma'am, I swear you have the wrong idea. Crystal is a good student and she seemed troubled lately. When I asked her what was wrong, she said she was depressed about Devianna, her little cousin that was kidnapped."

Jonetta was floored at the mention of the baby's name coming from the teacher. She stood facing the two with doubts about their story, but the conversation caught her off guard and she was forced to charge it off to being an overly protective mom. Still, a male teacher should never hug a female student.

"I'm so sorry. Maybe I did jump to conclusions. I just thought it was more than it appeared to be."

"It's alright ma'am, this happens all the time. I've learned not to argue with a parent about their child.

Crystal wrapped her arms around Jonetta's neck and hugged her. Then she turned to introduce the two.

"Mr. Robertson, this is my mother, Jonetta Barnes. Mom, this is my coach, Mr. Robertson."

"Pleased to meet you," Jonetta said cautiously, shaking his hand as she monitored his body language.

"I appreciate your stopping by and checking on your daughter. I wish there were more parents like you."

"Mm hmm," Jonetta replied skeptically. Her intuition screamed that something wasn't morally right with the hug, but dealing with her husband's nightmares and depression, she had her hands full trying to juggle the needs of her family. She was obviously missing something about Crystal.

The conversation ended abruptly with the ringing of the bell and groups of students filing into the classroom. With the feeling of guilt hanging over her, Jonetta nodded to the teacher and walked out the door.

She made it back to the car and called up Samantha for a sister chat. The phone rang twice, and then went straight to voice mail. Jonetta sat clutching the steering wheel, dreading the feeling of being deceived into believing the hug was innocent. Deep inside her mind, she felt as if her brain had failed to notify her what was really going on. She started the car and headed down the street, wondering if Crystal was telling the truth. She decided to head to her old stomping grounds.

When she arrived, Jonetta spotted the Benz parked in front of their old apartment. She whipped in next to it and looked inside, but there was no sign of Sam. On her way up the walkway, she recognized Samantha from a distance, posted up in front of D-Roc's building, looking just like Mama Dee from afar.

"Hey, Sis! I just called you. What's good, Roc?" Jonetta mouthed the closer she got to the couple.

"I must've left my phone in the car. What I do wrong, now?" Sam asked, touching on her pockets in search of the cell phone.

"Nothing that I know of, but whatever's in the dark will come to the light." Jonetta shot off quickly.

"What's that supposed to mean? I would never cross you in any way, Jay. You know that." Sam stood staring at Jonetta with a confused look on her face.

"Yeah, if you say so."

Baffled by the latest comment, Sam moved in closer to embrace Jonetta with her arms extended, but the love was misconstrued as ready for battle in the eyes of Jonetta. She backed up and drew both fists to the air like a boxer. When Jonetta drew back to take a swing, D Roc jumped between the two.

"Hold up, Jonetta! You are tripping!" He interrupted.

"She damn sure is, acting like she has a beef with me." Samantha echoed.

D Roc could see the stream of tears starting to roll down Jonetta's face. He grabbed her around the waist and walked off with her as she leaned her head on his shoulder. Samantha had no clue why Jonetta was tripping. She searched her memory for a reason that may have brought about a change in the bond the two had since the third grade. In her heart, she knew there was nothing she'd ever do to intentionally jeopardize their sister/friend bond. She traveled the length of the walk-way as she wondered where their future lay. Unable to contain herself, Samantha strolled over to where D Roc and Jonetta stood.

"Jonetta, this is me. What the hell's wrong with you?

"Look. I'm really going through something right now. Just leave me the fuck alone." Jonetta responded.

"I don't give a damn what you're going through. I'm your sister for life and don't you ever forget that! Why you call yourself posting up on me like you want to squabble? Samantha jumped into the Benz and sped out of the parking lot.
Jonetta just looked on as she drove away.

The plan of action was in place to get the snitch in the Thomas Jordan case eliminated. Time was of the essence and D Roc had failed to produce a hit man for the job. Sam sat on the edge of the bed and replayed the name and address of the hidden target over and over, replaying the conversation in her mind. She decided to GPS the directions, and then mapped the house on her computer to get a better visual of what she was facing. She jotted a few notes down on a pad and ripped the page off before heading back to her room. Sam slid back the closet door, reached up top for the black leather leg holster, and strapped it on.
 She clad herself in one of Mama Dee's old style dresses and a large church hat which curled over her face. Grabbing her purse on the way out the door, she went to the car to begin her fifty-one minute journey, according to the GPS.
An hour into the ride, Sam's phone rang. She looked over in the passenger seat and to her surprise, it was Jonetta. She answered immediately.
"Hello?"
"Hello," Jonetta responded, her voice cracking.
"What's wrong, Jay? Talk to me."
 "I'm just going through right now and I can't seem to gain control over my life."
 "I knew something was going on. I could see the distress in your face when you went off and tried to throw an Ali punch at me." Samantha joked to lighten the mood, but Jonetta was in no mood for laughter.
Sounds of whimpering could be heard through the phone.
 "I can't take this shit anymore! I'm tired."
 "Jonetta, listen to me. Slow your roll and talk to me. What's going on?"

"It's too much to talk about on the phone."

"Where are you, Jonetta?"

"I'm out rolling, scared to be at the house alone with Trevon."

"What? Has he been putting his hands on you?"

"Hell, naw! You know damn well I ain't going for that anymore! That ship sailed with Parnell Jenkins getting dirt thrown in his face, and Trevon don't want that. He's just been blacking out here late at night. I can't even begin to explain the shit I been going through the last few months."

"Look. I have to take care of some business right now, but meet me at my house in about two hours. If I'm not there when you get there, just go on in and wait for me."

"Sam, I'm sorry for going off on you. I just have so much on my plate."

"Jonetta, we have a bond that's unbreakable even by men. So there's no need to apologize. I understand you even when you don't understand yourself."

"I need your ear right now, Sis."

"Say no more. I'm on my way home."

Sam took the next exit and made a U-turn to head back toward the house. There was no decision to make when it came to her sister needing her. When she got home, Jonetta was parked with her head resting against the steering wheel. Sam whipped into the driveway and tapped the horn. They entered through the garage and Sam was alarmed at Jonetta's state of urgency.

"Damn, girl! It looks like you haven't had any sleep in days!"

"To be honest, I haven't been sleeping at all. I've been dealing with so much in that house from Crystal's bullshit, to Trevon fighting in his sleep; I don't know what I'm going to do! Sometimes I think he's on the verge of suicide. He's just not the man I once knew. I adored the ground he walked on, Sis. He hasn't been the same since we got back from Cali."

"What is he going through?"

"Trevon is fucked up. He can't seem to sleep at night. He's either drinking or fighting in his sleep."

"Get back to him in a minute. What the hell is Crystal's problem?"

"The problem started with him. Crystal was doing great in school for the first year and then somewhere halfway through her senior year, she started acting out. She sneaks on her phone all times of night texting and going on. I even picked her phone up one day and it had some young guy's genitals in a text message."

"I know you beat that ass real good!"

"What's that going to do? These days the child hollers abuse and the parent ends up on trial behind some bullshit."

"But we from the old school know ass beatings used to solve plenty of problems."

"Really? How much did it solve for us? We were involved in kidnapping, drugs, and murder!"

"I don't know what you're talking about. If Crystal needs some discipline, send her over here for a few months and I'll handle her ass."

"Sam, it's not about whooping the kid every time they make a mistake. You have to put yourself in their shoes and find a solution to the problem as a parent."

"Yeah, but a little ass whooping goes a long way. It will keep her in touch with reality. Girl, if you don't discipline her now, you may be crying over her dead body later on."

"I feel you. I just don't think beating on her will solve the deep-rooted problems she may have."

"Deep-rooted my ass! You and Trevon took her out of the projects and put her in a beautiful home with two responsible adults. She has anything she needs and more, including the hottest outfits at her upscale school. Her life has gotten nothing but better since she moved in with y'all. What else could a muthafucka ask for?"

"It's not about the materialistic things, Sam. That's just a cover up for what she might be feeling inside. The first few months after she moved in, she was so quiet and withdrawn. She wouldn't talk to men, period! Now, it's like she's trying to find her way with any and every man that'll accept her with open arms."

"Well, that's not good. That's why you took her out of the Jets, so she wouldn't turn out like her mother and the rest of them hoes."

"Oh, hell to the naw! I know that ain't Miss "I fucked every nigga in the hood" talking!"

"Oooh! You know you wrong for that!" Sam hollered.

"Girl, you know I'm just kiddin'. But to be honest, you have fucked

At least half the niggas in the projects." Jonetta burst into laughter.

"That's not what this conversation is about."

"Yeah, but it's all good. I hadn't had a good laugh in a minute." Sam reached out and grabbed Jonetta around the neck. The embrace felt like the good old days.

"I love you, Sis." Jonetta whispered as she hugged her sister tighter.

"Ditto, Chic. You know that goes without saying. So what about Trevon? You and brother-in-law have come way too far to give up now. The girl is probably looking for validation in men and needs some strong coaching. You know what she went through in California."

"Wait a minute! You said Crystal's problems began with Trevon! He's not hittin' on her, is he?"

"No! Nothin' like that. He's not hittin' on anything lately, including me! I'm going to try to talk Trevon into getting some kind of help and see if I can get Crystal back into counseling. I know she needs more than a beating to deal with the fallout from Boss."

"You sure can remember the shit that needs to be thrown out of your memory."

"What are you talking about?"

"I'm talking about the shit that happened on the west coast. Why you keep making reference to that?"

"I ain't thinking about that. I'm just talking to you."

"Yeah, but you never know who's listening. You taught me that."

The two embraced again and Jonetta got ready to go home and tackle her problems.

"Do me one last favor, Sam?"

"I'll do anything for you, Jay." Sam replied.

"Wipe the dust off my back so I can get my ass up and get moving forward, like a real woman knows how."

"It's all good. Everybody has down time. You know what Big Mama used to say. 'Minor setbacks cause for major get-backs in life.'"

"You sure are right about that. Hey, where were you headed when I first called you?"

"I was on a mission to take care of a little business."

"I apologize for taking you away from whatever you were doing to come and coach me back to sanity."

"You actually coached yourself, Jay. You held the key to every question you asked already in your head. And about the mission I was on? Nothin' comes before my half-breed princess." Sam smiled as she burst into laughter.

"Bitch, you trying to be funny?"

"Naw. I just had to get even."

The two burst into laughter simultaneously.

"Are you hungry?"

"Hell naw! You ain't going to fix me up none of that super love potion and have me trailing your every movement. I've already got two crazy ass people I'm dealing with, so I'll pass. You're the most dangerous of them all." Jonetta pointed her finger to the middle of Sam's chest.

"There you go acting like you want to clobber me with that right again."

"Get off the gas, Sam, and have a good day. I'll call you later."

"Bye, Jay. I love you."

"Love you more!" Jonetta called out as they headed outside.

Sam opened the garage door and Jonetta strolled out into the light of the day with her head up and ten toes to the ground, ready to restore order in her home.

Sam strapped the pearl-handled thirty-two caliber pistol to her leg and left, once again on a mission to eliminate the informant for the government. She traveled the distance without interruption, located the house, and parked a block away to keep the cheat from identifying her license plate. Sam spontaneously created a plan to catch the folks off guard if they were watching from a distance. She knocked on every door on the street asking for donations for the church's annual fund raiser, until she finally made it to where the snitch was being held. With her heart pounding, she unstrapped the small caliber pistol from her leg and slid it under the handmade donation plate with her finger on the trigger. She tapped on the door lightly to avoid alarming anyone, but there was no answer. She knocked harder, stepped back, and announced herself.

"This is Miss Violetta Shakur and I was doing a fund raiser for the church. Would you like to donate a dollar or two to the congregation at Mt. Carmel Baptist Church? It's down on Martin Luther King Blvd."

She waited for a response but there was none. Sam planted her ear to the door to listen for any sound of movement on the inside of the house, but there was none. She eased around to the side and peeked into the window through slightly torn shades. There, she spotted what appeared to be canned foods left on the table. Realizing the informant had been moved to another location and there was only a week until the trial was to begin, Sam faced a challenging dilemma. As she made her way up the street, she was confronted by an older woman waiting to give her a donation. Samantha slowed her pace to wait for the woman to walk across the grass with an envelope in her hand. Through the glare of sunlight, Sam could see the check inside.

"Ma'am, I apologize but the church has opted not to accept checks for this particular fundraiser."

"I beg your pardon? What kind of church do you worship at that doesn't accept checks?"

"Listen here, lady. It's not my call. These are orders that came directly from the Pastor himself." Sam looked up in time to spot the neighborhood watch truck headed in their direction. She abruptly cut the conversation.

"Drop it in the basket. Ma'am, if you have some concerns about how the congregation is run, then you need to take that up with the Pastor." Sam pulled the large hat down over her face and walked off. She marched towards the car holding her breath in every step of the way. The neighborhood watch guy passed by slowly with a menacing stare. Sam started the Benz and quickly left the area. She raced the entire way home and waited for Leon to come in.

An hour later he arrived and Samantha greeted him at the door with the news.

"I went to the location and the snitch has been relocated as if someone got a tip that I was coming."

"That's not it. Sometimes if they feel like the informant's location has been made or a neighbor spooks them for some particular reason, they'll up and leave in the middle of the night to keep the location confidential until trial."

"Damn. What are we going to do now?"

"To be honest with you, there's nothing left to do. They'll just have to face him."

"But you can't beat the case with the snitch's testimony. He was part of their daily operation at one time."

"I'll have to try to discredit his testimony and make it look as though his testimony was forced on him with a promise of less time."

"Do you think that will work?"

"Look. I've already gotten a million and a half out of this case. Whether it works or not is really not my concern," Leon said as he walked into the bedroom. Sam stood in the doorway, with a confused look on her face. She hoped she'd just taken it the wrong way. She thought more of Leon than that. Right then, she decided not to attend the trial.

The trial got under way on a cool Wednesday morning in September. Thomas Jordan and the other defendants were whisked into the heavily guarded courtroom and seated in the order of the indictments. They listened as Attorney Hale took the floor and discredited the testimony of each of the Internal Affairs agents that worked the case. Mr. Jordan sat comfortably at the defendants' table on the third day of the proceedings, confident that the half million in attorney's fees would be persuasive enough to sway the jurors' decision. The smirk on his face was soon wiped away as the reliable informant was led in by several deputy Marshalls, hands tightly gripping the firearms at their sides. Startled by the sight of the snitch, the overly confident man leaned over and whispered in

Leon's ear.

"What's going on? I thought that rat was going to be taken care of before trial?

"I apologize, but from my understanding, he was supposed to be taken care of a couple weeks ago. He was definitely not supposed to be available for testimony." Leon whispered back to his client.

"Is there any way to get the case postponed for a few weeks until I can get this?

Situation handled my mutha fuckin' self?"

"It's already gone past the time limit we had to get things in order. The judge is an asshole. He won't favor anything we come up with to buy more time unless it's about money, but I'll definitely give it a shot."

"Do it. That's what I'm paying you for."

Leon stood and asked the Judge for permission to approach the bench.

"Your honor, I'd like to ask for a continuance of this case."

"Counselor, can you please explain the reasoning behind your wanting to drag this case out when it's already been two and a half years since the defendants were indicted?" The judge responded.

"I want things to at least look good in the eyes of the defendants spending the money, Bob. I may be able to pull another hundred thousand or so out of the head agent if we can continue it for a few more weeks." Leon whispered back.

"Okay, but remember, you have agreed to give the prosecution this one."

"I know, and thank you again for talking the prosecutor into accepting that small "donation" on the Barnes case."

"No problem. Anything for you babe."

Leon turned and strolled over to his seat beside Mr. Jordan.

"I have him eating out the palm of my hands. We're all good."

The judge slammed the gavel down and made his announcement. "This court has been made aware that the defendant's legal representation is not adequately prepared to proceed at this time. Therefore, it's my decision to reschedule the proceedings until Oct 23rd at eight o'clock A.M. this court is adjourned.

Leon shook his client's hand, straightened his custom-made jacket, and exited the courtroom, winking at the wife of one of the defendants.

The weekend arrived and Jonetta called to see if Samantha would join her and Crystal on a shopping spree. Sam agreed to meet them at TJ Maxx and the three would go from there.

When Jonetta walked into the bedroom preparing to leave, she encountered Trevon standing in the doorway of the bathroom, butt ass naked, stroking his manhood.

Annoyed at first that he would be doing that instead of making love to her like he used to, she saw the faraway look in his eyes and had sympathy for him instead. "Is everything alright, Babe?" she asked.

"They gon' be coming soon. I'm going to stay ready."

"What are you talking about, Trevon?"

He pointed towards the slightly open curtain and started to shake.

"Babe, calm down! Everything is going to be fine." Jonetta grabbed Trevon under his arms and pinned her breast to his chest, staring directly into his soul through his eyes. His pupils were not visible.

"What's wrong, Babe? What's the problem? Talk to me, Trevon! I'm your wife, the one person that vowed to be by your side through thick and thin! Good or bad!"

Trevon did not react to his wife's words. He started to chant unfamiliar phrases with his arms spread out wide. Jonetta clawed her husband's torso as she continued to stare at him in disbelief.

"I am the almighty one and that's why they come to take me away."

"Trevon, have you lost your damn mind? There's no one coming for you."

"Prepare yourself for war!" Trevon responded, his eyes as big as golf balls.

Jonetta shook her head in sorrow over the way her husband had handled himself since returning from California. What had happened to the Trevon she used to love? The one who had saved her life and risked his own to save another? The level-headed one who took care of the family? She knew the answer. He'd been gone a long time. And if he was ever going to come back, she had to do something drastic.

Sam faced a terrible dilemma. The Trevon she now lived with was lost. He was paranoid and possibly suicidal. At her wits end with his schizophrenic behavior, she felt she had no choice except to have Trevon committed to a psychiatric institution for treatment of suicidal tendencies and manic depression. That was the diagnosis after the first few days of testing.

Of course he fought them off when they arrived to pick him up. He thought they were the ones who'd been coming after him for weeks. He ripped off his clothes and lunged at one of the EMT's like a madman, but they were skilled enough to bring him down and handcuff him to a gurney. It didn't take long for the drugs to kick in as Jonetta looked on in horror. She briefly thought of Devon, and how disappointed he would be to see his twin acting this way, reduced to a babbling psychopath. But after a night of tears, Jonetta pulled herself together for the sake of Crystal, who needed her now more than ever. Since the day Trevon saved her from Boss and took her in, he had been her hero.

Having Trevon committed was the hardest decision Jonetta had ever had to make. But at least she had done something. And she had done it out of love. She was tired of watching him deteriorate more and more each week. The break was hard for Jonetta, but with Trevon's sleepless nights, she'd been alone in bed for months already.

The first few days he was away, Jonetta managed to hide the whereabouts of her husband to friends and family, but after a period of time, it became apparent to the others that Trevon was MIA. Jonetta decided to throw a fish fry to get their close friends and family, the people that mattered most, at the house to explain to them what they were going through.

Friday evening rolled around and everyone invited was at the house, Sam late as usual. Jonetta's hospitality was at its finest. She had prepared a feast for kings. They enjoyed the fish, fried potatoes, and Caesar salad, and then they moved into the spacious living room for a round of cocktails. Jonetta had to work up her nerve to take the floor and release the secret that she had sworn she would take to her grave.

"Can I have everyone's attention please? I personally consider every one of you here today more than just close friends. You're family. And I value your individual opinions. I know that I can tell every one of you anything without being judged, and I could've trusted you to take it to your grave."
Jonetta swiveled her neck and covered her face with both hands to hide the tears starting to flow from her cheeks.

"Let it go, child. Let it out and get it off your chest," Mrs. Jenkins blurted out, as she sympathized with the hurt Jonetta was feeling.

"I'm so sorry. I'm a little emotional right now. Y'all please forgive me."

"It's alright, sister. We are here for you." Sam chimed in nervously. She had never seen her best friend choked up like this and she found a knot growing in her stomach with worry.

"I know. I know. I just need a few minutes to gain my composure," Jonetta replied, waiving one hand in the air as the other wiped away the tears.

"Take your time, little sister. We have all evening. I don't have to be in court until 8 A.M. in the morning." Leon replied. Sam slapped his arm playfully, but with enough force to let him know that she thought his being facetious was not well-timed. All eyes were on Jonetta's every movement as her bottom lip quivered. She sucked in a deep breath of air and nervously began.

"I may as well be a big girl and get this off my chest. When I was in the hospital with injuries from Parnell, I was forced to have a blood transfusion to replace blood I lost during that last beating. For years, I rolled through with no complications of any kind. Then, a couple years ago, we were delighted to finally find out that Trevon and I were going to have a baby. We were back and forth with my doctor on a weekly basis; making sure things were all good before we told anyone. But on one particular visit, my world was turned upside down. The doctor came in with a folder in his hand and said he had some bad news. The test results were back from the lab and it showed that my blood was H.I.V. positive. I was torn to pieces, so I asked my doctor to do a second test because that blood must've been contaminated in some way. I wasn't willing to accept the results. My stress affected the baby and I lost it. Jonetta scanned the room to see their facial expressions one by one. She wanted to see their reactions to her announcement. She noticed the terrified look on Leon's face. "When Trevon's test came back and he, too, had been infected with the virus, he started tripping, immediately claiming we were going to die. I tried to explain to him that we needed to consult with my doctor to see what our next course of action would be, but he was so adamant that we were doomed to die."

The only two dry eyes in the home belonged to Carson and Mr. Hale. Jonetta paused to catch her breath and locked eyes with Carson. His demeanor told a story that said somehow, someway, he already knew. Jonetta thought back to the early morning when they were leaving the hospital after Cynthia died. When Trevon managed to over-exert his already weak immune system, he insisted on riding with Carson, explaining that he wanted to talk to him about something. Jonetta would get around to asking him about that later.

Carson straightened up in his seat and stared sympathetically at his cousin's wife while the others looked away in total disbelief. Leon sat thinking that as close as Jonetta and Samantha were, they had to have crossed paths or shared a threesome together at one time or another. He wondered if he was at risk.

"I realize that most of you are probably confused that I hid this from you for so long, but fearing that people would pass judgment on our pitiful condition, Trevon and I thought it was best to keep it to ourselves. I thought he was handling it well, but lately he's been going off the deep end, so bad he got scary to live with. After the last conversation we shared, his words were so crazy and actions so bizarre, I realized that the Trevon I knew and loved was no longer there. I really struggled with having to have him committed to a mental hospital, but there was nothing else I could do. He needed professional help if I was ever going to get him back. I love my husband, and there's nothing that I wouldn't do to make him happy, but he has allowed our situation to define who he's become. The Trevon I knew was just gone." The tears streamed down her face again as she lowered her head, waiting for their reactions.

The Boss Take Over

Mrs. Jenkins, Parnell's widow, was the first to speak. She and Trevon had become close after his father's death. She had helped them get back on their feet financially, and a strong bond had developed with Jonetta as well. Mrs. Jenkins was more of a mother to Trevon than his own had been. She understood life better than any of them.

"First of all, Jonetta, I think you're a wonderful person and a devoted wife to my son. You need to understand that life will have its ups and downs, but with the strength and courage of a lion, you must struggle to overcome your past. There's no need for you to have ever felt like any of us would pass judgment on you or Trevon, if you really thought of us as your family. Real families don't act like that. What we do is join together collectively, create a plan and follow through. I'll be the first to say that I'll be here for you every step of the way with whatever you need --- an ear to listen, a place to stay, or money. Just name it." Then she held her arms open for Jonetta to come in.

She moved forward and embraced her mother-in-law, resting her head on her shoulder. Ingrid joined in and all the women, including Crystal, huddled together while Mrs. Jenkins led the prayer. Jonetta felt a sense of both relief and rejuvenation, that a terrible burden had been lifted.

Jonetta hugged each of her friends, pausing in front of Sam.

Sam stood with her hands on her hips and her bottom lip protruding.

"What's wrong, Sis?"

"I'm angry! We're supposed to be your family and we're just now finding out about this?"

"Sam, listen. I didn't want to alarm any of you with my health issues, so I kept it to myself. I know it was probably selfish of me, but I was really stressed when I first got wind of it. I didn't know what to do. On top of all that, Trevon was in my ear talking stupid like we were just going to keel over and die. I didn't want to worry anybody.

"I understand that, but don't ever keep something as serious as a life or death situation from me, of all people! I'm down with you through sickness and death like we married, Jonetta Sharell Barnes! I love you with everything in my soul and I vow to see to it that you and Trevon are okay, at least until I'm ready to leave here and then y'all are on your own!" Samantha rolled her neck playfully and the tension evaporated. She smiled, wiping the tears away from her sister's face with the back of her hand.

Ingrid explained being HIV positive was not the death sentence it had been twenty years ago. There were programs and treatment at the hospital where she worked, and she'd make sure Jonetta had access to everything that could save their lives. Mr. Hale offered his financial assistance as a support package.

Mrs. Jenkins glanced at her watch and realized the time.

"Well, young people, this has certainly been an eventful evening, but it's past my bedtime. I'm going to get on out of here and I'll see you another day."

"Thank you so much for coming and sharing your wisdom." Jonetta replied as she walked Mrs. Jenkins to the door.

"What's the name of the place Trevon is in?

"He's at Patton State Hospital right now. Crystal and I went to see him Monday.

"I'll get up there next week and have a talk with him. I need to see how he's doing for me."

"That would be wonderful. He needs all the support he can get right now."

Mrs. Jenkins wrapped her arms around Jonetta one more time and whispered in her ear.

"Everything is going to be alright. When you look for strength in the Creator, He will make sure you know that He is at your side."

Jonetta raised her head from the older woman's shoulder with tears in her eyes as she spoke. "You're the rock that I lean on and the inspiration I seek. I really appreciate you for coming."

"No problem. I'd do anything for you and Trevon."

Mrs. Jenkins was the epitome of strength in a woman. She exuded the confidence of a billionaire with the meekness of a child of God. One by one, the others departed, and when the last person crossed the threshold of the home, Jonetta closed the door and slid down the wall feeling sick to her stomach. From birth, she felt as if she had never been given a chance to excel, and now she was dealing with a possible death sentence from living with the wrong man. Why had she been so stupid? Sleeping with anyone who came with a luxury lifestyle! Her life had been cursed for generations and she needed to figure out a way to break the curse before it took her all the way down.

When she raised her head, she felt the heat of someone standing over her. It was Crystal, hovering over her with tears in her eyes.

"Mama, I'm so sorry for all the things I've put you through. I want to apologize for my actions these last few months. I was being selfish and looking for attention. I was afraid I would lose you when I first saw Trevon starting to go through his depression. I felt like no one was listening to me. You seem trapped in your own world, more worried about what he thought than what I was going through. I was mad because I thought you were worrying more about him than me, the child you claim to love. I started acting out to get your attention."

Jonetta raised her head and looked into her daughter's eyes. . She was amazed at the soothing words that came from the young woman's mouth. She was thankful that Crystal finally understood what she was going through and that she was no longer out of the loop.

"Crystal, you're a wonderful daughter and I'm proud to have you as a child."

"I haven't been so wonderful lately, Mama. I haven't been honest or caring. But from now on, I promise that I will be. We can get through this together."

Crystal actually seemed relieved that Trevon was gone. Jonetta embraced the young woman with the love of a strong mother. She hadn't known that feeling since Mama Dee died.

Chapter 11

Samantha rolled out the bed, planted both feet on the carpet, and disappeared into the restroom. After showering, she headed to the kitchen to get Leon's breakfast going. Thirty minutes later, his meal was prepared and sitting bedside on the TV tray.

"Babe. Babe!" Samantha shook the sleeping man several times until he woke up mumbling to himself. Leon turned over, wiped his eyes and then stared up at the metal tray.

"Damn! You got me loaded down this morning."

"When you take care of Mama like last night, I handle my mofo business for you in the morning, Daddy." Sam winked, did one finger snap in the air, swiveled her naked frame around, and switched off towards the kitchen. Leon was impressed with the feisty young kid from the projects. He admired how she was able to transition her thinking from the empty environment she was raised in, and with the help of her two best friends, she eventually turned a potentially disastrous life into a work in progress. She was still a little rough around the edges, but determined to get to whatever level in life she was reaching for at the time. The lawyer's only reservation was not being able to take the young woman to the Annual Lawyer's Conference as a couple. Samantha's verbiage was off the chain, on the breath-taking sharp at a moment's notice, and he feared she'd be perceived by his peers as more of a clingy client rather than a potential wife. He was cool with paying a few bills and keeping her his little secret.

Sam returned to the bedroom cuffing two hot cups of coffee and sat on the edge of the bed.

"So what are your plans for today?" Leon asked.

"I may ride over to Ft. Worth. I need to check on my sister and that daughter of hers. Then I'm going to run by Patton and check on brother-in-law. Why? What's up, you need me to do something for you?" Samantha twisted her upper body looking directly at Leon.

"Why didn't you take care of that little business we talked about?"

"As I told you before, I went to the location and evidently the folks got wind that I was coming. They moved the snitch to another spot before I could get to him." Sam looked up at Leon for a response of some kind, but there was none. She sipped her coffee in the silence.

Feeling the heat of her thoughts, he took a deep breath and dropped his head, shameful of the words soon to escape his mouth. "I alerted them to move him. I need his testimony to seal your ex's fate," Leon mumbled.

Sam sat staring at the top of the Leon's dome, slightly recalling the slick comment he'd previously made concerning the high profile case. It was the second time she felt jitters in the pit of her stomach. She decided to satisfy her curiosity and address the situation face on.

"What do you mean seal my ex's fate?"

"Sam, I had to do what I felt necessary to protect you from him ever hurting you again."

"That's the lamest thing I ever heard, Leon! First of all, you weren't even in the picture when he was around and what do you mean protect me from my ex?" I've been able to protect me all my life!

"That's news to me! You don't remember crying on my shoulder telling me how he used to put you in a headlock and grapple your ass to the floor like a wrestler until you passed out?"

Sam could feel the anger in his voice and the wrinkles on his forehead without even looking at him. She felt a sense of betrayal that she had not anticipated. She thought they were so close. After all, they'd been sleeping together for months. She couldn't believe that she was hearing these words from Leon's mouth. Questions filled her thoughts as she speculated on the real motive behind Leon's shady decision to turn against his client.

Unable to contain herself, she demanded, "Is that the real reason, Leon, or is it about the money Ernie has hidden that you and the judge have yet to get a hold of?"

"What money?" Leon countered, resting his head against the headboard.

"The millions Ernie and his crew stole from the banks. Don't play games with me, Leon! I was in the courtroom." Sam replied.

"See, Sam. That's what turns me on about you, that bulldog tenacity to get to the bottom of things." Leon cooed, attempting to smooth things over. He continued to dodge the issue by avoiding a direct answer.

"That doesn't answer my question at all."

"Okay, okay. You want the truth?"

"Ya damn skippy! If you happen to have any of it left in you!"

"If you insist on having the honest truth, I'll give it to you. It's a little of both, the case and the money."

"A little bit of both my ass! You all about the money and I can see it in your eyes! But you can bet your bottom dollar you aren't going to play me! I will be all the way down or nothing at all!"

"What do you mean all the way down?"

"What part of that don't you understand, Leon? I want to be down with all the money coming in on behalf of my ex, as you call him, or I will get a message to him that you and the judge got some fuckin' shit going on. Remember, you, by your own admission, don't plan on defending him to the best of your ability. If I'm going to stand behind the scenes knowing the real scoop on how this trial is fixed to play out, I will be compensated well for my disloyalty." Samantha yelled disgusted with the predicament Leon had put her in.

Sam lived for the underdog and nothing could ever change that about her. She'd get paid if it took a bloody massacre.

"Samantha, I have a business partner I need to consult with before I can promise you anything."

"Yeah? Well, I'll tell you this much. If Judge Bob doesn't see fit to cut me in on the cash cow you'll have poppin', then he'll mysteriously come up missing along the way, along with the others that called themselves going up against me!" Sam replied eyebrow arched to match her sneer.

Leon was caught off guard by the gun hoe threat that slid off Sam's tongue. He wanted desperately to respond, but his vocal chords were on mute; no words came out.

Sam stomped out of the room feeling the warmth of a hole being burned into her back, and then she giggled to herself at the fear apparent on his face. She dropped the dishes into the sink and returned to the room with a smile on her face. The better side of her bipolar illness kicked in and her mood suddenly shifted. Leon threw the covers back to get out of the bed, and Sam hurried over to make sure his house slippers were under his feet before they hit the carpet.

"Damn!" Leon exclaimed. You change faster than a whore changes her drawers."

"I wouldn't want anything to happen to the man I depend on to hold me up through the storm." Sam cooed in her best Southern belle dialect. Leon draped his naked body in his cashmere robe and headed toward the restroom. Sam caught a glimpse of the dirty look out of the corner of her eye as she made her way to the closet to retrieve her clothes. Agitated by the actions of a man that had taken an oath to provide honest legal counsel to his clients, Sam slipped into her blouse and jeans. Grabbing her purse off the granite counter-top, she rushed to her car, slamming the door behind her.

Her thoughts rambled wildly in her head. "This mutha fucka think I'm just some stupid ass bitch from the ghetto! He got me fucked up. I ain't dumb by no means! But if he wants to play pussy, he'll be the one getting fucked down, real swell."

Sam pulled out of the garage and intentionally backed into the front of Leon's Porsche Cayenne, mangling the grill on contact. She got out checking the rear end of her Mercedes for damages, but they were minor. She darted over to the front grill of the Porsche and chuckled before getting back into her car and peeling rubber out of the driveway. She felt a sense of satisfaction for the ones getting played.

A half hour later, Leon tapped the garage door opener to let himself out. Hot enough to cook an egg on at the sight of his caved-in grill, Leon reached for his cell phone and dialed Samantha's number. But to his dismay, the phone went straight to voicemail.

At his wits end, he decided to leave message "love note."

"Bitch you playing with fire and going to get your little ratchet ass scorched."

He went back into the house to gather up his things. It took less than an hour to fill his trunk and backseat with the expensive suits and shoes he wore in court. Leon then ripped down every piece of clothing Sam had hanging in her closet or folded on the shelf. He grabbed the garage door opener from the sun visor and threw it back inside, as the garage door slowly rolled down behind him. "It was good while it lasted," he said to himself.

Sam arrived at Jonetta's just in time to catch her leaving. She climbed into the backseat and leaned against the window.

"Hey, yawl." Sam said in a somber tone.

"Well aren't you the happy camper this morning?" Jonetta asked.

"Hello, Aunt Sam."

"Hi, Crystal. How are you doing??"

"Great! I'm back on the A-B honor roll, but this time I'm number two and shooting for the top spot." Crystal replied with enthusiasm.

"Now that's what I'm talking about. Always shoot for the top spot. In life, two is not a winner and nobody remembers three."

"I am. I had a few quirks to work through, but I'm all good now."

"That's okay. We all have gone through some rough patches, but the wisdom in us is the key to continuing on beyond the struggle. And when it comes to men, never trust a man that has to apologize more than twice in a conversation."

"I really appreciate your wisdom, Aunt Sam. I will keep that in mind."

"I was introduced to most of what I'm telling you by your mom, many years ago." Samantha replied.

Crystal looked over at her Jonetta and smiled, happy to be in the company of two best friends that should've been joined at birth.

After dropping Crystal off at school, Sam moved to the front seat. As soon as she moved up, Jonetta demanded, "What's your problem?

"You remember when you called and asked me to meet you at my house to talk?"

"Yeah. . ."

"I was on my way to smoke the witness in Thomas Jordan's case, but I turned around to make sure your ass was alright. Anyway, a couple of days later, I rolled back out there to see if I could get at him again, only to find out that the witness had been mysteriously relocated. I felt like something was wrong with that picture, but I never said anything to anyone besides Leon. When I tried to get a reaction out of him, that bitch stayed quiet. Then, earlier this morning, I woke up feeling all loved and shit, gave the little dick mutha fucka his props for nubbin me down, and he had the nerve to ask me why I hadn't taken care of that business he and I discussed since the trial was starting again soon. So I told him the snitch had been relocated and there was no way to find out where he had been moved to until they were back in session and I could get an earful on a possible new location. I looked up, Sis, and this bitch got his head tucked between his legs, talking bout he alerted the folks to get him out the house."

"What the hell did he do that for?"

"I don't even know! Your guess is as good as mine."

"'Sounds like he was trying to get you caught up."

"I do know one thing. It's all about the money with him. He doesn't plan on representing the man or his crew on the cool. I heard him the other day talking to the judge on the case, and it seems like he's already planned on throwing this case to the prosecutor."

"Damn! That's how the legal system is working these days?"

"Hell! You act like shit has changed! It's always been all about the Benjamin's! You remember Trevon telling you Mrs. Jenkins had a million and a half prepared for the defense team to pick up the appeal, if our murder case hadn't turned out the way it did? Coming out of Parnell's camp, she knows the price of freedom comes with lining the pockets of them thieving ass folk's downtown."

"Are you sayin' Leon is crooked?"

"That mutha fucka will fuck a dry turnip to get the juice to stream."

"Girl, yo' ass is crazy!" Jonetta replied, laughing at Samantha's latest comment.

"That's what he thinks, evidently."

"Yeah? Well, you know what to do to show him different. Work what Mama Dee taught you on him."

"I got his ass covered like a grandma quilt, Sis."
Jonetta pulled into the parking lot of Patton State Hospital. The two exited and strolled the short distance from the car to the entrance of the hospital. Jonetta dreaded watching Sam see Trevon for the first time since he'd been so sick.

"If this place didn't have this looming fence towering over the buildings, it would look like a four-year university from the outside." Sam said, staring up at the barbed wire on top of the fence.

"I can get you admitted at the front desk if you'd like me to," Sam joked.

"Shit, I give these mutha fuckas seventy-two hours and they'd be putting me out for failure to comply with the program. You know, they say them real crazy men have really long dicks to make up for the good sense they missin."

"Bitch, please! Where'd you get that lie from?"

"Shit. Ain't we visiting brother-in-law up here?"

"See? That's exactly why I had my fist cocked back on your ass the other week. You always got some foul shit coming out your mouth," Jonetta said, staring at Samantha.

"You know I keep it poppin'!"

"Don't get popped fucking around in the wrong backyard."

When they reached the entrance, Jonetta pushed the button on the intercom.

"Your name, please?"

"Jonetta Barnes."

"The name of the patient you're here to visit?"

"Trevon Barnes."

"What's your relationship to the patient, Mrs. Barnes?"

"Damn! They need to know your whole life story to visit somebody around here?" Sam whispered to her sister.

Jonetta stared back at Sam and without moving her head; she shifted her eyeballs upward to indicate the camera was watching their every move.

"What is your relationship to the patient, Ma'am?" the clerk repeated impatiently.

"Oh, I'm sorry. I didn't hear you. I'm Trevon's wife." Jonetta stated proudly.

The door buzzed and the two entered the reception area cautiously. Feeling trapped, Samantha halted as the doors closed loudly behind them.

"Come on, Sis." Jonetta encouraged as she noticed how wide Sam's eyes were.

Sam crept up to the glass window and peeked inside.

"Get off the window, Sam. They're looking right at you."

The door to the visiting room opened and Jonetta enters and pulled Sam in behind her.

"Mrs. Barnes! Are you back already, with another patient?"Mrs. Nellums joked.

"No, we are here to visit my husband, but I'll keep you posted. She may change her mind by the end of the visit and want to stay," Jonetta reciprocated.

"If I do, we're all going to be roommates, so y'all make the decision. The ball's in your court!" Sam said, looking first at the older woman and then back at Jonetta. She didn't crack a smile.

"Bring your ass on, Sam," Said Jonetta under her breath.

The two found an empty table close to the vending machines and seated themselves. Within minutes, Trevon was escorted to the visiting room partially robed in a moo-moo gown. He was smiling from ear to ear at the sight of their familiar faces.

Jonetta, however, was outraged when she saw her husband's backside exposed and his hair matted down on his head. She immediately headed in the direction of the guard standing with Trevon. The closer she got, the more infuriated she became, now gawking at the bulge of his penis on the rise clearly seen through the hospital gown. Wrapping her arms around him to close the distance between them, she was momentarily traumatized from the feeling of the hard penis pressed against her abdomen.

Sam was speechless at the pitiful sight of her long-time friend. She didn't know whether to make a joke in her usual style or cry over the sadness of the scene. Feeling the "You'd better not" stare of Jonetta, she chose to stifle the comment fighting to escape her mouth. Instead, she just shook her head and said his name, "Oh,

Trevon."

"Excuse me, Sir," interrupted Jonetta. "Can I please get you to take him back to his room? He needs to be dressed properly. He shouldn't be exposed like this. And comb his hair while you're at it," Jonetta whispered over Trevon's shoulder.

"What's wrong with what I have on, Devianna? I mean Jonetta?" Trevon inquired.

"Look. We have company today so don't start this bullshit and embarrass me again, Trevon."

"I ain't doing nothin' wrong." Trevon responded, shaking his head.

"Have you taken your meds today?" Jonetta demanded.

"What meds? I don't need no damn meds!" Trevon screamed as Samantha looked on in horror. She didn't believe her eyes. She had never seen her brother-in-law so confused and unpredictable. She desperately wanted to just run over and squeeze the warrior back to reality.

The transportation guard was called back and the patient was whisked away to his room. He was redressed and forced to take his medicine. A half hour later and highly agitated by the commotion of the last few minutes, Trevon returned to the visiting room fully clothed with his hair combed. His big smile had evaporated with his good mood.

"What you bitches want?" Trevon blurted out.

"Excuse me, crazy man! Who are you calling a bitch?" Sam responded without a thought of how her words would affect a person in Trevon's state of mind.

Trevon wavered as if his equilibrium was out of balance. "Who the fuck is you calling crazy? You two bitches have been killing mutha fucka's for years!"

"Calm down, Trevon!" Jonetta said forcefully. "This is your wife you're talking to!"

Sam was further taken back when Jonetta had to explain who she was as if they had just met. Realizing too late the need to be cautious of the words coming from her mouth, Sam looked her brother-in-law directly in his eyes, but Trevon swiftly turned his back, denying her access to his thoughts. She reached out to embrace the troubled man, but he pushed her hands away and posed to fight. With a fierce look on his face, Trevon backed up and started to curse at Sam, causing a scene. Onlookers fretted at the sight as Jonetta stepped between them, trying to calm them both down. By this time, Trevon was bouncing on his toes like Sugar Ray Robinson, poised for a fight.

"Code 10! Code 10 to the visiting room!" The guard screamed into his radio and seconds later, the door to the rooms swung open. Several guards rushed in searching for anyone fitting the description of the "fight in progress" distress call. The team of six quickly located Trevon, posted up with a stunned look on his face. Two oversized members of the S.O.R.T. team cuffed him and led him off to a solitary confinement cell. For everyone's safety, Jonetta's visit was terminated and the two were asked to leave the facility immediately.

Furious at the way things unfolded, Samantha vowed her loyalty to her childhood friend. "Oh, my God, Sis, he really needs our help! I didn't realize he was that bad off!"

"He's been exploding like you just saw him or blacking out for about six months. I told you I haven't been getting any sleep, too scared to be in the house with him alone when he's like this."

"Brother-in-law or not, I'll put something on his ass to get him straight, if he thinks putting his hands on you is cool." Samantha threatened.

"He hasn't made the mistake of putting his hands on me, but he has gotten my attention with the late night drama sessions."

"What the hell?" Samantha argued as she got into the car.

"Sis, I'm just going to be honest with you. I've been woken up many nights with Trevon either standing over the bed butt ass naked fondling himself, or he's up in the media room drinking shots of Jack Daniels and calling out Devianna's name."

"You think his obsession with finding his niece is causing all this?" Samantha queried.

"Girl, that man is beyond obsessed! One morning I woke up and when I didn't see him in bed, I got up and tipped up to the media room to check on him. Trevon was sprawled out on the carpet with a pistol next to his head. Thank God I had unloaded all the weapons in the house a few days before. The first time that happened, there was actually a bullet in the chamber. By the Grace of God, it was one slot past the firing pin."

"What did you do?"

"I did what I felt was best for everybody. I got up and got Crystal out of the house before he woke up.

Jonetta fastened her seatbelt and Sam did the same, mouth wide open.

"I had no idea he was in such a state of mind, Sis."

"It's pretty severe, Sam, and I don't know if I can keep waiting to see if he's going to get better."

"Now hold up, Jonetta. You took the vow for better or worse in your marriage. You can't just give up on your husband when he needs you the most."

"I've done all I could hoping to see a change in him, Sam, but lately, I feel like he's left me with nothing but emptiness on the way to hatred. Sometimes I doubt if he'll ever recover. He may never be the same again, and I have to face that."

Samantha scratched the top of her head as she leaned against the window in deep thought.

An hour later, Jonetta pulled into her driveway and opened her garage.

"Are you coming in, Sis?"

"What time is it?"

"You can't ask a question with a question."

"Says who? Whether I come in or not, depends on what time it is."

"Damn! You make things so difficult! It's10:45 in the morning. Now what do you have to do?"

"I don't have to be anywhere in particular this morning. I just had to get out of the house before I killed Leon's ass. I'm sure he's gone by now, though."

"Take your time and play your position. He'll show his true side soon enough."

"Shit! He already showed it when he sent me on a mission I could've been caught up on for free."

Sam got out of the car and slammed the door behind her.

"Damn! why you slam my door so hard?"

"I'm sorry, Jay. You know I didn't mean to slam the door."

"You need to settle down and learn how to channel your energy into something positive."

"I'm positive as hell about one thing only! Either he cuts me in on the money or I'll be forced to end up killing both him and that scandalous ass judge he has in his pocket."

"Sam! Calm your nerves! Revenge isn't always the best way!"

"Who else is going to take care of us better than us?"

"Ingrid." Jonetta said with a smile.

"Don't be funny. You know what I mean."

"I know you didn't go there as much as your ass jokes around." Jonetta replied as she pulled into the garage.

Sam unlocked the Mercedes and threw the deuce at her sister as she pulled off.

Jonetta waved back, then lowered the garage door and went into the house. After dropping her purse on the kitchen counter, she noticed the red light blinking on the answering machine.

"Three messages. Damn! I wonder who this could be." Jonetta said to herself as she pushed the play button.

"Mrs. Barnes, this Mr. Mitchell, the senior counselor at Alexander Hamilton Prep Academy. I was calling to inform you that Crystal Barnes was not present in any of her classes today. Crystal is really a good kid but it seems that she's easily distracted by some of the more popular young men of the school. I am available for conferences on Tuesdays and Thursdays between the hours of ten and four. I can be reached at 817-284-2447. Thank you. I look forward to hearing from you."

The recorder beeped, signaling the end of the first message.

The second message caught Jonetta off guard.

"Yeah, it's me bitches! You mutha fuckas thought y'all got away with something, but you didn't! Be on the lookout and keep your domes covered."

Jonetta was unable to catch the distorted voice and for good reason. She rewound the message and listened intently to every word, but she was still unable to put the voice with a name. Shaken from the ominous message, Jonetta pushed the button and listened to the last message.

"There can be no me without you, so I've decided to leave here.

By the time you get this message, I will have taken my life. I can't live with lies anymore. People will look at us like we have shit on our face if we're ever exposed. The pain is just too much. I know you're probably thinking "he's stronger than that," but to be totally honest, I have no strength at all without the woman I would kill for. I've let my brother down and I've let my family down. I'm a man without honor. So I'm going to be with Devon, wherever he may be. I love the times we spent together and I will miss you all: Mom, Carson, Crystal and Ingrid, even Sam. Goodbye forever, my love.

Chapter 12

Jonetta rushed back to the kitchen to retrieve the cell phone from her purse only to find there were several missed calls from Patton State Hospital. She punched in the ten-digit number and got a busy signal. Frantically, she scrambled back to the recorder to listen again while dialing the number back. The phone rang twice and a deep voice bellowed out over the line.

"Hello, Patton State Hospital. This is Officer Jackson speaking. How may I assist you?"

"I need to be transferred to the Cherokee Unit, please!"

"Is this a personal call?"

"I'm calling about my husband. I received a voice mail stating that he was going to kill himself and I really need someone to check on him!"

"The patient's name?"

"Trevon Barnes. I need to get somebody to go and check on my husband without all the questions! Please!"

"Please hold while I transfer you."

The phone is transferred but tit rang several times before it was answered.

"Cherokee Unit. Mrs. Nellums speaking."

"Mrs. Nellums? This is Jonetta Barnes. I need you to check on my husband. He left me a message saying he was going to kill himself!" she cried frantically.

"Calm down, Mrs. Barnes. I called you a while ago to let you know the shift officer found your husband in his cell with a sheet tied around his neck hanging from the grate. He got him down in time to save his life."

"Oh, my God! Where is he now?"

"He's been transferred to the rubber room where he was stripped of his clothing and anything that he could use to further harm himself. They will monitor his every movement by camera for at least the next twenty-four hours."

"When can I see him?"

"He's heavily sedated now. Let's observe him for a day. You can come tomorrow morning around ten. I'll make sure he's available."

"Thank you so much, Miss Nellums. I'll be up there at 10:00 sharp."

"I'll see you then."

Jonetta ended the call, and then dialed the number to the school.

"Alexander Hamilton Prep Academy. How may I help you?'

"Can I speak with Mr. Mitchell, please?"

"Hold on one second, please."

"This is Robert Mitchell speaking. How can I help you?"

"Hello. Mr. Mitchell. This is Jonetta Barnes, mother of Crystal Barnes. I received your message earlier and was returning your call. What did you mean; Crystal wasn't in her classes today?"

"Mrs. Barnes, Crystal has either been late or skipped class every morning for the last three days and I was wondering if you were aware of it."

"Late? Skipping? I've been dropping her off every morning on time."

"Well it seems that somewhere between you dropping her off and her getting to class, she's been taking a detour along the way."

"I'm on my way up there right now." Jonetta replied, having heard enough.

She grabbed her purse and headed out the door. Her mind was filled with all kinds of visions of Crystal getting high or acting out with boys. She tried to calm herself down until she could get to the bottom of Crystals bad behavior. Damn! She'd thought that problem was solved. A few minutes later, she arrived at the school, parked, and decided to investigate the whereabouts of her daughter on her own. She rounded the building and eased up on a group of boys passing around a joint.

"I know y'all are not smoking weed on school property!" Jonetta accused. The teenagers scattered away from the scene but not before one of them were snatched by the back of his jacket.

"What do you want from me?" The youngster yelled out, almost suspended in mid-air.

"Do you know a young lady by the name of Crystal Barnes?"

"Who?"

"Crystal Barnes is her name."

"Only Barnes I know is a senior that calls herself "Chocolate Swirl.""

"Do you know where I can find her?"

"Ain't no telling 'bout Swirl. She may be in class or she could be trailing one of the jocks. She's off the chain!"

"What period is this?"

The boy looked down at his watch to check the time.

"We're supposed to be in fourth period now, and I know she has first lunch. So she should be coming this way in a few minutes."

"Where does she usually go for lunch?"

"Most of the time she hangs out here with some of the guys when she comes out the building."

"Where do they go? Who are they?"

"Ma'am, listen. Just take me to the office and report me. I'm through with the questions."

"I never had any intention of taking you anywhere, but you better get your life together before you end up in the rubber room at Patton."

The young man stared in amazement, frightened by her warning. Jonetta let the trembling youngster go and he disappeared faster than a cockroach when the lights are flipped on. She headed towards the bleachers and stood behind them to await her daughter's arrival.

It wasn't long before Crystal come strolling out of the building surrounded by a group of young boys, pants hanging well below their waists.

"These hoes betta respect that Cali life around this bitch or get dealt with." Crystal yelled out to one of the boys. She gave him "dap" and continued on towards the back of the building. When she turned the corner, she halted dead in her tracks, setting her eyes on the woman standing alone beside the bleachers. Crystal desperately tried to hide behind one of her friends when she saw her mother's profile, but Jonetta stepped out just in time to lock eyes with her errant daughter.

"What the hell you doing, Swirl?"

"Just keep it moving, man. That's my mom over there by the

bleachers lookin' this way."

"It looks like she found you. Here she comes. You in trou-ble!" he teased.

Jonetta charged the crowd and gripped Crystal around the neck with her left hand, slapping her about the head with the right.

"You know better than this Crystal! What the hell is your problem?" Jonetta demanded, now clutching the teen by her blouse.

"You're not my mother! You didn't raise me! Now let me go!" The disobedient teen shouted back as she snatched loose from her grip.

"Oh, no, you didn't go there!" Jonetta lost all composure and threw her mommy skills out the window as she stepped out of her shoes and fired a right at the angry girl, missing by inches.

"Damn!" someone yelled from the crowd around them. Others laughed, covering their mouths and pointing. Students had gathered behind the building watching the show like it was *Jerry Springer*. Feeling the heat from the attempted punch, Crystal stomped off in the direction of the office with Jonetta on her bumper screaming at the top of her lungs. It was more than embarrassing for both of them, but Crystal's humiliation was as strong as her anger at Jonetta.

"I knew you were a coward!" Jonetta yelled at Crystal.

When she reached the door to the office, Crystal turned the knob to enter and was plummeted over the head with an overhanded right. The sassy teen let go the door knob and hit the ground face up, eyes wide open. A teacher spotted the commotion and motioned the secretary to call the school police to the scene.

Jonetta was arrested for domestic assault and led away to the county lock-up. Crystal was taken to the nurse's office and given an ice pack while she slowly regained her bearings. The school had no choice but to call CPS. Several students had gathered outside the office, laughing and retelling the story, co-signing the George Forman punch.

Jonetta was booked into the county detention center on domestic violence with bodily injury to a minor. Her bond was set at ten thousand dollars. Hours into her stay, she was granted her free phone call to make arrangements to be bonded out. She called Sam's cell phone but it went straight to voicemail after the third ring.

"Damn! Where is your ass when I need you?"
Jonetta made a second call and Ingrid picked up.

"Hello?" Ingrid answered, confused about who would be calling her from the Tarrant County Jail.

"Ingrid, this is Jonetta. I need you to contact a bondsman to get me out of jail."

"Jail? What are you doing in jail, Jonetta?"

"Crystal's counselor called and said she was skipping class, so I went to the school to check on her. I caught her mobbing the courtyard like she was the toughest thing walking and she was talking shit at the same time. So I tested the talk and she ran off like the coward I knew her to be."

"So what did you go to jail for? How much is the bond?

"The bond is ten thousand, and they took me to jail 'cause she slipped and fell at the door to the principal's office."

"She slipped and fell? Did you have anything to do with the slip and fall?"

"It wasn't me! It was the overhanded right that knocked her to uncertainty."

"Jonetta, you know you can't do that on school property! You're really gonna have problems with her now! She's gonna hate you for humiliating her like that!"

"The Bible say's if you spare the rod, you spoil the child! I wasn't spared, so neither will she be, living under my roof and for damn sure, not on my watch."

"You know the law has changed since we were brought up. The difference between discipline and child abuse is a very thin line these days."

"Damn the law! Either you discipline them now or they'll be beating you across the head later on in life!"

"Girl, I know what you mean."

"You're fading out, Ingrid. What did you say?"

"I'm at the front door of the hospital so the reception is bad."

"Okay. So you're at work?"

"I was on my way in, but I'll go in here now and let my boss know that I have some business to take care of and I can work on-call if he needs me. What time does Crystal get out of school?"

"She's usually coming out the door around 3:45. If you don't see her ass, go looking for her because she's been on some bullshit lately."

"Alright, cool. You know I'll check it out if things don't look right. I'm getting ready to call Sam now to see if Leon can make your bond for you. Then I'll go and get Crystal from school. She and I need to have a heart to heart."

"Thank you so much, Ingrid. I knew I could count on you."

"No worries. I'll make it happen for you one way or another," Ingrid assured her friend.

"I really appreciate that."

"That's what unconditional friends are for, Jonetta."

"Alright. The guard is waving at me like my time is up. I'll talk to you later, hopefully when I'm out of this cell."

"Just hang on, girl. I got you."

When Jonetta hung up, she was escorted to the doctor's office to see if she required medical attention. The nurse took her blood pressure and her temperature, and drew a sample of blood to keep on file for DNA purposes. Once the nurse finished, an officer took her back to the holding cell.

Ingrid put in a call to Samantha, but there was no answer. She tried again with the same results. So she walked to her boss's office to inform him of her situation.

"I would like to be put on-call for the rest of the day if possible. I have a few personal issues I need to take care of."

"That's fine," he replied. It's been fairly slow around here today, thank God. Is everything alright?"

"I'm good. I just need to pick my niece up from school this afternoon. My sister ran into a few unexpected problems, and asked me if I could help her out."

"Alright. You will be on-call for the rest of the day.

"Thank you so much, Dr. Dubois," Ingrid replied.

She turned and took the elevator back up to the third floor of the parking garage. After sliding into the driver's seat of her Fiat, she paused for a moment, gripping the steering wheel and thinking back to how emotionally torn she was when Jonetta revealed that she and Trevon were H.I.V. positive. She just knew from that day on Jonetta would find the strength within and walk the straight and narrow path to eternal life, but now here she was calling from jail after a public brawl with her daughter.

She wished her two best friends could somehow be persuaded to get their lives back on track, but deep inside she knew suggesting they change would be more of a challenge than she had the patience or energy to deal with. Ingrid realized that time was of the essence, and the further they continued into their madness, the further south they were headed. She felt that neither of the two had truly taken advantage of the second chances that God had given them. They were taking their blessings for granted.

Although Carson claimed he had no recollection of the events that had taken place, Ingrid was sure that something terrible had happened in California. After Cynthia took her own life and her baby was never found, Trevon was bent on vengeance with Sam and Jonetta right behind him. It became more apparent to her when Jonetta and Trevon were so adamant about adopting the teenager, even though her mother hadn't taken care of her for years. Now there was every chance that they would lose Crystal to CPS. She had seen it happen so many times before at the hospital. Both nurses and teachers were required by law to report signs of abuse. Ingrid didn't want to worry Jonetta any more than she was already, but she was in no position to fight for Crystal in jail.

Ingrid slumped against the steering wheel, exhausted from looking for ways to coax her friends back into responsible, productive citizens. She decided to run her plan of action by Jonetta to see how well she received it and then move on to Sam later. Her thoughts were interrupted by the sound of her cell phone vibrating. She reached in her bag and grabbed the phone.

"Hey. Sam. I called you earlier to see if Leon could get Jonetta out of jail."

"Jail!" she yelled. What the fuck is she doin' in jail?"

"Crystal was skipping classes and Jonetta went up to the school. They got into it and Jonetta tried to beat her in front of the principal so they called the police. Can you talk to Leon?"

"Fuck Leon! That bastard packed all the shit he could grab and tore his ass in a hurry, just like a coward when he can't face the music." Samantha continued her rant through the phone.

"Calm down, Sam. This is Ingrid."

"I know who the hell I'm talking to!"

"Evidently you don't, Sam, because you are yelling at me like a child." Ingrid replied with agitation.

"I'm sorry. I'm just going through some bullshit right now," Sam said with more control.

"You're the one leading yourself on that journey, Sam."

"What the hell are talking about?"

"Sam, I've been trying to get you and Jonetta to understand that life doesn't owe either of you a dime and you need to continue to grow in wisdom in order to change with the times."

"But we are changing with the times! We got nice cribs and badass cars like we always talked about when we were growing up."

Sam, it's not always about the material things you value so much. That's just a cover up for the pain that most people hide behind. The reality of it is you have to begin to love yourself as a person first."

"I do love me, girl. I love me more than anybody. That's why I make sure I'm looking good."

"Listen, Sam. There's no way that either of you can truly say you love yourself and you continue to put yourself in harm's way time and time again."

"Look. If you're talking about what happened in California, that was a spur of the moment thing. We didn't go there with the intentions of killing anybody, but it turned out that we had to do the damn thing right."

"Things turned out the way they did because no one had the courage to try and work them out. Trevon was feeling guilty about what happened to Cynthia and the baby, and you all just jumped on the bandwagon half-cocked. Can you honestly say it was worth it?"

"Hell, yeah! It was worth it! We all came back including

Carson, and the people that got hurt didn't matter!"

"It's time to grow up, Sam, and get your priorities in order. You're getting ready to turn thirty next month, and you're still just as bull-headed as the day I met you! You're just in these streets with no sense of direction. You're always blaming somebody for what's wrong in your life!"

"I know where I'm going!" Sam retorted. "I'm going with the flow and I make the money flow in the process!"

"Yes, for the time being. But as I was saying earlier before being bombarded with your negativity, Jonetta called about a half hour ago from the county jail. She needs to be bonded out."

"How much is it?"

"I don't know. The charge is assault on school property and endangering the life of a minor.

"If that's the case, it's going to be about a grand to raise her."

"Do you have it?" Ingrid asked.

"Easy. I can make the whole bond several times over."

"Well, well. I'm glad you're in a position to help Jonetta when she needs it. And it's good that you're so generous. But she might need more than money. You know the school is required to call the Department of Children and Family Services when things like this happen. Jonetta might have a fight on her hands getting Crystal back.

"Well, that's not good. But I'm ready to do whatever it takes. Like Mama Dee taught me, I stay ready to keep from having to get ready."

"Sam, I want you to always remember, it's not how much you make but what you learn on the journey that really matters."

"Yeah, right. There you go with all that preachy stuff. I'll call this other bail bondsman I know to see what he can do."

"Thanks, Sam. You know, you should listen to yourself sometimes. You should have been a lawyer.

All Ingrid could hear on her phone was the dial tone. Sam had hung up.

Chapter 13

As Ingrid pulled out of the garage into the light of the day, she was instantly revived from the subdued mood caused by the problems of her loved ones. She sped across town just in time to get a front row parking spot in the students' pick up area. She pushed the seat back and waited in anticipation as she carefully chose the words she would say to Crystal if she hadn't been taken by CPS. Ingrid didn't want the troubled girl to feel like she was talking down to her, but that she was a loving motherly figure and friend offering her sound advice. The sharp-witted woman devised a plan to get Crystal to trust her and not hold back what was bothering her so much.

When the school bell rang, kids disperse in all directions. Ingrid got out of her car and leaned against the fender to get a better opportunity to see Crystal come out, but the flow of students quickly dwindled without any sign of her. Not one to give up easily, Ingrid entered the building and briefly looked inside each classroom she passed. At the end of the hallway, she paused in front of the restroom, took a deep breath and enters the girls' side searching each of the stalls. But there was still no sign of the teen anywhere. She rounded the corner to the boys' side and the awful stench of urine hit her square in the face. Holding her nose, she kicked the first stall open and moved towards the second, when the rattling sound from a belt buckle could be heard behind her.

"Crystal, is that you?" Ingrid asked, but there was no response. With the brute force of an NFL linebacker, the fearless woman forced her way into the large stall to investigate the sudden movement on the inside. The door slammed against the stall divider and Ingrid stood face to face with a young man, mouth wide open, pants at his knees and gym shorts in hand covering his manhood.

"I'm so sorry," Ingrid said weakly as she backed away from the stall, ashamed of her intrusion. She exited the restroom and paced the hallway, looking over her shoulder every step of the way.

The Boss Take Over

Suddenly, out the corner of her eye, she spotted the back of a young girl in the last classroom on the left. Slowing her pace, Ingrid moved closer to the classroom window, hoping to see the girl's face. What she saw shocked her. It appeared to be her niece's head bobbing up and down! Ingrid snatched the door open and stepped in the room with authority. Her nostrils flared when she found Crystal on her knees with an older man's penis in her hand. Her loud roar, "Oh, hell naw!" startled both the coach and the teen out of their lustful escapade. Crystal let loose the penis and leapt to her feet as if nothing was happening. But the damage was done and it was about to get real ugly! Outraged at the sight, going on, Ingrid rushed towards the older man and clobbered him about the head with her fist as he desperately tried to buckle his pants.

"You are one dead son of a bitch, you horny old bastard!" Ingrid yelled as he scurried away like a cockroach.

Ingrid grabbed Crystal by the arm, but the sassy teen snatched away from her grip, and all hell broke loose! Ingrid slapped her in the face with a hard right, leaving an imprint on her cheek, but the impact didn't stop Crystal one bit. With bells ringing in her head and her equilibrium slightly unbalanced, Crystal lunged forward to further challenge Ingrid's authority. But the fragile teen was no match for the one-time project Original, turned nurse. Crystal was met with an Ali blow to the face, two to the body, and a Tyson uppercut which sent the teen flying through the air for the second time that day. Ingrid walked over, grabbed the unconscious teen by her collar, and drug her to the door.

Slowly coming back to life, the girl staggered to her feet, and with Ingrid manipulating her like a puppet master. She linked arms with Crystal and helped her to the passenger side of the Fiat. She opened the door, pushed her on to the seat, and buckled her up.

A few minutes into the ride Crystal woke up and looked around at the unfamiliar scenery.

"Where are you taking me? Is it the same place where Boss kept me hid out for days?"

"What the hell do you call yourself doing Crystal?"

"What do you mean?"

"I mean having some nasty ass old man's dick in your hand, that's what the hell I mean."

"I just want to be loved by somebody that cares about me, not someone that took me in out of guilt.

"What are you talking about?"

"Jonetta and Trevon only took me in because they killed my aunt Paulette and felt the need to adopt me. They wanted to ease their guilt."

"Why do you say that, Crystal? They didn't kill anybody."

"You weren't there, so you don't know the whole story! They came to California to a place call the Chocolate Swirl and killed Boss and one of his girls in the house."

"How do you know this?"

"I was there! I saw them do it! They took my aunt and then she disappeared!"

Crystal was telling her what Ingrid had suspected, but she didn't know for certain. She didn't want to.

"So you've been holding in all this anger all these years?"

"Yeah, and I'm going to the police."

"Police? Are you out of your mind? We don't do police in this family, Crystal!" Ingrid blurted out as she imagined all the fallout.

"But I'm tired of the lies and deceit! I'm tired of covering up what's been going on in that house!"

"What's been going on that's so horrible?"

"I've been getting raped, ever since I moved to that house!"
Ingrid was stunned. "Raped?" she questioned. "Raped by whom?"
Crystal was ringing her hands. "There's only one man that lives there. Who else could it be?" she replied in a monotone.
Ingrid stared at the young woman in total disbelief. She could never imagine her childhood friend being capable of something this bad.

"Are you saying Trevon has raped you ever since you moved in with them?"
Crystal took a deep breath. "I'm saying ever since I've been in that house, there's been some type of abuse inflicted on me. He started out by standing in my door way naked and once he saw I was scared to say anything, he started feeling on me. He started caressing my breasts and then fingering me. One night I woke up and found him standing over me jacking off. I wanted to scream at

the top of my lungs, but he put a knife to my neck and told me if I screamed, he'd take my life like he did my Aunt Paulette for talking too much. I was scared to death. I covered my eyes and cried as he spread my legs open and stuck his penis inside me. I begged him to get off me, but he wasn't trying to hear anything I said. I didn't know what else to do but go along with it."

Ingrid could only sit staring through the front window, shaking her head. She had heard plenty of stories like this at the hospital, but never from anyone she'd known personally, never from anyone in the family.

"After that, he got completely out of hand," Crystal continued. "The moment Jonetta crashed for the night; he'd call me to the media room and force me to suck his dick until he came. I got so used to the routine that I just went along. I thought that's the way he showed me he loved me since they'd taken me in.

"I didn't want to go back to the projects. I had my own room here and nice clothes and spending money. My mama was dead, my aunt Lakeisha on drugs, and Big Mama was getting' too old to take care of anybody, so I did what I needed to do to survive. If it meant giving head, so be it. At least Trevon wasn't as mean as Boss.

"I can't believe this shit you're telling me. Where would Jonetta be all this time?"

"Most of the time she'd be asleep. But sometimes, I think she knew. She'd come to the door and listen, then go back out real fast, as if she didn't see what was going on."

Ingrid could not fathom what Crystal had just told her. "Are you saying Jonetta knew that Trevon was molesting you?"

"She always acted as if nothing was ever wrong and we had a happy family in a perfect world. She more or less kept the flow of material things coming, so that on the surface it appeared to be something it really wasn't. But I think deep inside she knew what was happening to me and that's why I have no respect or love for her at all."

"Crystal, I can't believe what you're saying. This can't be right. Jonetta couldn't know what was happening and allow it to go on! These are the people that took you in. You can't bite the hand that feeds you!"

"So am I supposed to sit back and continue to get raped? Continue to just let Trevon and Jonetta get away with this? Aunt Ingrid, is that what you're saying? How would you feel if this was happening to your daughter?"
Ingrid was caught off guard by Crystal's accusations. She sat at the red light in a total dilemma of what to do next, until her cell phone rang and pulled her out of her deep thoughts.

"Hey, girl." Ingrid answered, trying to keep the trembling in her voice from coming through. She was not in the mood for conversation.

"Did you find Crystal?" Sam said loudly into the phone.

"I have her in the car with me now, and we're on our way to the apartment."

"I thought you we're coming to the house after you took care of your business."

"I had intended on doing that, but I made a detour. I need to stop by the house first before I do anything. I may not even make it to the bank."

"Don't worry about the bond being made. I got in contact with a lady that works up at Pearson's Bail Bonds and she assured me that they could get Jonetta out in a few hours. All I need to do is get the money to their office by five P.M. I'm on my way there now."
Ingrid took a deep breath, summoning the courage to question her decision to get Jonetta out of jail after hearing what Crystal just told her. She needed time to figure out what to do.

"Are you sure you want to do that right now?"

"What the fuck are you saying, Ingrid? You know damn well she needs to be free. Why wouldn't she?"

"I really need to talk to you as soon as you drop the money off at the bondsman. Stop by the apartment when you finish."

"I will. I need to talk to you as well, Leon done tripped out and I'm going to have to handle his ass real severe."

"I hear you, Sis, but this is really important so get here as soon as you can."

"Alright, alright. I'll be there as soon as I can," Samantha replied, sensing the urgency in Ingrid's tone.

Ingrid pulled into her covered parking space and turned off the car. She looked over at Crystal, amazed at what the child had been made to endure at the hands of two people she considered her best friends. It was as if they were living an entirely different lifestyle than what appeared on the surface. It was one filled with sick twists and perverted fantasies involving the innocence of a minor. Ingrid decided that if the young girl's story is validated in any kind of way, their friendship of twenty-three years would come to an abrupt end.

"It's okay Crystal. Come on into the apartment." Ingrid said as she wipes the tears away from the young girl's cheek.

"Do you believe me? Or are you going to hurt me like everyone else?"

"No one will ever hurt you again, not on my watch." Ingrid said as she leaned over and wrapped her arms around the nervous teen, holding her firmly against her breast. After several minutes in the car, Ingrid convinced Crystal to come into the apartment where they could finish their conversation. She thought a cup of tea might relax them both.

A half hour later, there was a knock at the door.

"Who is it?" Ingrid yelled through the closed door.

"It's me. . . Sis."

"Come on in," Ingrid replied wearily. She didn't know how Sam was going to react to Crystal's story. And she had to tell her right away. They had to decide what to do about it.

When Samantha opened the door, she was surprised to find Crystal curled up next to where Ingrid had been sitting. She was wrapped up in a comforter like a baby.

"What's going on in here?" Sam snapped. "It damn sure ain't cold enough outside, for you to be all bundled up!"

"Sit down, Sis." Ingrid said, patting the edge of the couch

"Oh, hell! What's really going on?" Sam exclaimed.

When she spotted the tears on the child's face, she had a funny feeling some shit was in the works. She was eager to hear what was so important that Ingrid patted on the end of the couch like she was directing a dog to sit. Sam sat down, crossed her legs and double-stacked her antennas for greater listening, all while still in zero tolerance mode.

"Well, to start off," Ingrid began nervously, "when I went to pick her up from school today, I caught her in a very compromising position with one of the teachers at the school."

"Hold up right there! Were you on your knees again, givin' one of them old mutha fucka's head at that school?" Samantha demanded, looking Crystal directly in the face.

The teen turned away and dropped her head, not wanting to reply to the question. Ingrid stared at Samantha to let her know she thought the questioning was too harsh, but she quickly recognized the teen's withdrawn gesture as a sign of deception.

"I asked you a question that requires an answer, Crystal!" Sam continued to intimidate.

"I don't want to talk about it! Ask your homeboy/brother-in-law and see what he has to say about it!" Crystal snapped back.

"What are you lying about now?' Sam fired off.

"That's what I wanted to talk to you about, Sam, Ingrid intercepted. "When I picked her up, she started telling me how when she wakes up, Trevon is standing in her doorway butt ass naked, playing with himself. She says he's been molesting her ever since she's been living in the house."

Samantha was shocked at the accusation. She couldn't believe it. But she did recall having a conversation with Jonetta about how Trevon ended up being committed for standing in the doorway ass naked, stroking his manhood. She now wondered if her sister was really covering for Trevon by saying it was her he was stalking, when in reality it was the child. Torn between her loyalty to Jonetta and Trevon and her natural tendency to protect a child, Sam wasn't sure what to think of the Crystal's accusations against her people. The only thing that kept her from leaning towards the child's side was their third grade vow of loyalty that held them all together. Sam was committed to their vow and no one had the ability to change that, not even Ingrid.

"So you claiming Trevon's been fucking on you?" Why are you just now saying something about it when you get caught in the act of servicing another man's dang-a-ling?"

"I was afraid and I still am," Crystal whimpered. "Trevon is a killer! You know that."

"I don't know where you get that from, but you best keep your mouth shut or it'll be permanently shut for you!" Samantha threatened.

"What? Just like my Aunt Paulette?"

Samantha stormed out of the room to gain her composure. The child knew too much and she had to do something about it fast before she, too, was caught up in a murder case.

"Crystal, I hope for the sake of your well-being that you are telling the truth about everything because if not, a lot of people will be hurt," stated Ingrid as she placed both hands on Crystal's shoulders.

"I ain't gonna lie about something as serious as a man raping me."

"Well, I'm on your side and we're going to get to the bottom of all this mess as soon as we pick Jonetta up from jail."

"No!" Crystal protested. "Please don't say anything to her right now! I'll be in a lot of trouble when she finds out I told someone the family secret."

"The hell with the family secrets! I will get to the bottom of this accusation 'because that's not the way I roll!"

"Please, Aunt Ingrid! You don't have to live with them! Trevon could kill everybody in the house the way he is now. And I don't know what Jonetta's gonna do!

"You can stay here for a few days until I sort through the issues. I'll have a serious talk with Jonetta and I'll even speak with Trevon's doctors."

"Thank you!" Crystal said with a sigh of relief. "Can you take me over to the house so I can get some clothes and stuff?"

"As soon as Jonetta calls, we'll be on our way."

Samantha entered the room with a look of disgust. She was angered that the young girl had the nerve to try to put her sister and brother-in-law in the mix. She grabbed Crystal by the collar, picked her up, and pinned her against the wall.

"You think your dusty little ass can come around us after twenty something years of friendship and make us believe what you say is the gospel? I don't believe a word you say!" Samantha stood close enough to smell fear on the young girl's breath.

She let go of Crystal's collar, straightened it with both hands, and then patted her in the face. "Things are going to be alright. You just need to keep your mouth shut and quit spreading those lies, kiddo. If not, I'm sure I can arrange for it to be permanently shut, not just for conversation, but from the very air you breathe."

Crystal stood frozen, back planted against the wall, and eyes buck terrified out of her wits. She knew Sam wasn't the one to make empty promises. She had heard about her reputation in the projects all her life.

"Now, tell Aunt Ingrid the truth and ease her feeble ass mind, because I see you have her all rattled up and ready to change positions in the middle of the game." Sam sneered.

Crystal paused, and all Sam had to do was look her in the eye.

"I'm sorry for making up those things about Trevon and Jonetta, Aunt Ingrid. I was just trying to get somebody to listen to me and understand what I went through when I was held hostage. Boss did horrible things to me and I felt ashamed then and I still do. But I learned that men like that stuff and that's why I do it. I just want them to like me.

"Crystal, you don't have to be defined by your past. We all have a past, but some of us shake it loose, grow from our experiences, and better ourselves." Ingrid responded with relief as she darted her eyes at Samantha.

"But you can't have a past being a nurse, can you?"

"You can do anything you set your mind to, Crystal. And yes, I do have a past. But, I chose to use my past as a stepping stone, to better the future I am headed for. I've been involved in crime, and I went to prison, but no one outside of family knows about my conviction besides the people I trust, which now includes you."

"You've been to prison?" Crystal asked in awe.

"In my earlier years, I, too, made mistakes that I was ashamed of until I prayed on it and gave it to God. Crystal, you cannot continue to hoard in things of your past. You must release them and move forward."

"Look," Sam interrupted. That's enough of all this introducing our past into evidence."

"Kids today need to know the truth, Sam. We as parents sometimes give the impression that we've been model citizens all our lives, when in fact, if we discuss some of the things that may have hindered us in our youth, then maybe our children could get a better understanding from a firsthand perspective." Ingrid testified.

"I disagree with you, Ingrid. I don't feel like a kid should have a play-by-play movie of my life."

"I didn't say a full account of your life, Sam. What I said was we should teach children our values and morals early on by showing them examples, to give them a method of survival for a lifetime, not just for the moment." What's that expression? 'Give a man a fish; you feed him for a day. Teach him how to fish; you feed him for a lifetime."

The front door opened and Carson entered, tossing his jacket across the couch next to Samantha.

Glad for the distraction, Ingrid went up to her husband and hugged him. "Hey, Babe. How were things at the studio today?"

"What's going on in here? Did I just walk into some girl drama?"

"No, just a little girl talk, nothing in particular. I think we have the whoa's all straighten out now, right Crystal?"

"Yes, Ma'am. Everything is fine." Crystal quickly replied.

Carson looked at each of the ladies wondering what was so important they had to cut it off when he came through the door. He decided to let it go for the moment and shifted the thought to his memory bank for pillow talk later on with his boo.

"I talked to Trevon about an hour ago and he said they were going to let him go this weekend. I didn't expect him to be getting out so soon. " Carson said. The look on Crystal's face was one of sheer terror. She was frightened to the core. She latched on to Ingrid with a vice-grip, tightly locking her arms around her.

"Come on, child! Quit faking and let's go and get your mother out of jail." Samantha coaxed as she tugged on the child's arm.

"I don't want to go back over there! Please don't force me to! I'm scared to be in that house with Trevon!"

"Crystal, quit all the drama and getting folks upset! You told the truth when you admitted you lied, so why are you changing your story now?"

"I was scared. I just said what you wanted me to say, Aunt Sam."

"Come on here, child. Nobody believes your lies but you, unfortunately, and that's the way it'll probably be till you die."
Ingrid stood in the doorway of her apartment with Carson watching over her shoulder in disbelief as Crystal was forced to the car against her will.

"Something's not right with that picture," Ingrid said as she ducked under Carson's arm and headed to her bedroom. Carson shut the door and followed close behind.

"What's going on, Ingrid?"

"I don't feel like talking about it right now, okay? Just leave me alone."

"Leave you alone? What kind of a statement is that? What's going on with Sam and Crystal?"

"Just leave me the fuck alone! That's what I said! Now what part of that don't you understand?"
Carson was shocked at the tone of her voice and the meanness of her words. He had never heard a disrespectful word come out of her mouth. Carson ended the standoff by walking away, not wanting to make things any worse. Even though he'd just gotten home, he left the apartment to give her some space.

Samantha arrived at the detention center and found the bondsman standing outside the tall brick building waiting on his client.

"Stay put while I go in and meet with the bondsman to see where Jonetta will be released." Samantha ordered Crystal.

"Can I turn on the music?"

"Sure. Just don't blow out my speakers." Samantha cautioned as she got out of the car. She raced across the main street to beat the oncoming traffic of downtown.

"Hey! Mr. Pearson?" Samantha shouted as she got closer to the older man.

"Hello, Miss Williams. Mrs. Barnes should be released within the hour. I signed the bond about a half hour ago and that's usually about how long it takes for clients to be released afterward."
Pearson pulled up his sleeve to check the time on his Movado watch. After firing up a cigarette, he leaned against the wall. The

sound of car horns blaring through the air caught both of their attention.

"Who in the hell are they blowing at?"

"I don't know. People are road rage crazy these days. It may have been someone running across the street while the traffic was coming. It sounds like it came from the side street right through there." Pearson pointed his index finger with the cigarette still lodged between his thumb and middle finger. He finished his cigarette, dashed it to the ground, and walked up the stairs to the prisoner release center with Samantha on his heels.

After twenty minutes or so, several prisoners were released at the side door, but there was no sign of Jonetta. Samantha looked over at the bails bondsman, but he just shrugged his shoulders as if to imply that he didn't know what the holdup was. Then finally, after everyone had come out and been picked up, Jonetta exited the facility with a hospital mask strapped around her mouth.

"Damn, girl! Why it take you so long to come up out of there?" Sam said, frowning at the mask on her sister's face.

"I got classified and then moved to a quarantined cell for the security of the population." Jonetta replied, with her head hung down towards her chest.

"It's all good, my sister! I'm by your side no matter what happens."

The lawyer stared intensely at his client, realizing what Jonetta meant. He tossed the paperwork on the table, out of his immediate reach.

"Sign on the line where the X is."

"Thank you for bonding me out, Sir. I'll be sure to check in each week."

"Not a problem, young lady." Mr. Pearson said curtly.

Jonetta stood up to give the bondsman a hug, but he took a step back, clearly ignorant of the facts about HIV. She could sense that he was trying very hard not to touch her or anything she'd had her hands on. She knew that feeling all too well.

Samantha grabbed her hand and the two walked off towards the car.

"I'm parked right over here, Samantha pointed towards the car.

"Did Ingrid make it to the school in time to get Crystal?"

"She's sitting over in the car listening to music."

They reached the car and quickly noticed that Crystal was nowhere to be found. Sam looked inside and found the keys still dangling in the ignition.

"I thought you said the Crystal was out here."

"She was out here when I left. I told her to stay put until I got back. I can't believe she left my Benz sitting here with the keys in the ignition. We could've been walkin' home."

The two anxiously searched the parking lot for the missing girl, but they couldn't find any sign of her. It was if she had never been in the car.

"Where could she have gone, Sam?"

"Your guess is good as mine, Jo. I left her here listening to music like I told you. She couldn't have gotten too far, though."

Samantha eased into the front seat and motioned for Jonetta to join her. She pulled out of the lot and shifted to a slow cruise, making her way up the block as they diligently searched for the missing girl.

Crystal peeked out from behind a trash dumpster, and headed in the opposite direction.

Chapter 14

The weekend arrived and Trevon was still on lockdown. His life outside the mental institution was put on hold pending further prognosis from a specialist. According to the case worker's report, his future was unclear. He could be harmful to himself if the prescribed medicine wasn't taken properly. Trevon faced a major crisis in his life with the H.I.V. and it was consuming his world.

Trevon stood in anger, looking out of his window contemplating a way to get back into Jonetta's good graces. He knew his actions of the last few months made him unworthy to be called a husband, but he would somehow redeem himself and get back in before it was too late. For days, Trevon watched the laxness of the second shift staff as he went about his daily routine. So he devised a plan to escape the facility during the last meal of the day.

Every evening, each of the institution's doors was unlocked for chow. Trevon stepped out of his room and fell in line with the rest of the crazies, head hung low. He wanted to make sure that when his escape attempt took place, he would only be detected by the count of patients, not by his face.

He eased past the first of the staff members and made it up the hallway into the chow hall. He watched their every movement with intensity. Trevon quickly scarfed down two servings of the shit on a shingle and headed out of the mess hall, under the pretense that he was going back to his room. Although he was classified as a J-Cat, Trevon wasn't one of the ones who needed to be led to and from his destination. He got halfway down the hallway and looked back at the staff monitoring the more severe patients. He realized they were consumed in their own conversations and makes his move. He dipped off into a utility closet and pulled the door closed behind him, paranoid of being caught up and sent to the twenty-four hour observation room.

He knew once chow was over and the last of the zombie-like people were escorted back to their perspective areas, the hallway would be clear of any staff. He sat quietly thinking of where he would go to call Carson to pick him up since when he had no money. It was too late to turn back now. He would just have to figure out his next move once his escape was complete.

Trevon peeped out of the closet and spotted the maintenance man working on a light fixture. He kept the door cracked until the man had finished his work order. He began to push the cart towards the back door and Trevon sprang into action. Trevon sprinted towards the door as it flung back to close, and bolted out of the facility through the staff parking lot.

Hearing the loud bang behind him, the maintenance man looked back and saw the patient running for dear life. He quickly re-entered the facility and alerted the authorities of the escape. The darkness helped Trevon's getaway go well. And by the time the alarms were sounded, Trevon was already a mile away.

He laid low until he figured out his next plan. He needed to call Carson to come get him, but he had no money. He thought about standing in front of the store and panhandling for change, but he knew that may jeopardize his freedom. Trevon decided that the best thing for him to do was walk to Carson's apartment. He couldn't go home. That's the first place the police would look for him.

A couple of hours later, exhausted from the walk, Trevon made it to Carson's apartment. He knocked on the door and sat on the steps to rest. After a few minutes, a deep voice bellowed from behind the door.

"Who is it?"

"It's me, Cuz."

Carson opened the door and stood shocked to see his cousin sitting on the steps.

"Damn, man! How the hell you get out the cuckoo house?"

"Look, no time for questions right now. I need to come in and get cleaned up," Trevon said as he walked through the apartment door.

"Is anybody following you?"

"Not over here, but they will be looking for me at the house. Where's Ingrid?"

"She's at work. She'll be in by midnight. Let me get you some clothes."

Carson went into his bedroom and came out with a jogging suit.

Trevon showered and the two sat up for hours talking. A few minutes before midnight, Ingrid entered the apartment and frowned at the sight of Trevon sitting on her couch. She rushed into the bedroom, slamming the door behind her.

"What the hell is wrong with her, man?"

"Shit. Your guess is good as mine. Let me go see."

Carson walked into the room and shut the door behind him. In minutes, Trevon heard the two arguing. He wasn't sure if it was about him, but he started to feel the burden of coming between the two. He slipped on the jogging suit and stepped out on the porch to get some fresh air. He sat thinking about how he had destroyed his family by sneaking around and stalking Crystal's every step.

Within minutes, Carson stormed out of the front door and slammed it. Seeing the frazzled locked on his cousin's face, Trevon took a deep breath and prepared for the worst.

"What's her problem?"

"I don't know, but if she feels like she can give me an ultimatum when it comes to you, she got me fucked up."

"Cuz, I didn't come here to cause a problem between you and your girl. I can go someplace else if she has an issue with me being here."

"Fuck what she talking about! You can stay right here until things cool down!"

"Thanks, Cuz. That's what family's for."

"You don't have to tell me, I'm down like four flat tires."

Carson hugs his cousin's neck and assures him that he has his back to the fullest. The two re-entered the apartment and Trevon flopped down on the couch to rest. Carson walked into the bedroom and Ingrid stopped dead in her tracks.

"Have you taken care of your business yet?"

"And what the hell is that supposed to mean, Ingrid?"

"It means that I refuse to be caught up in anymore bullshit, Carson. Trevon needs professional help, not you to enable him."

"What are you talking about?"

"Trevon is not supposed to be out of the psychiatric institution. He's a sick man. What did he do, breakout the place?"

"Look, Ingrid. Trevon is my cousin and I will not sit here and allow you to talk about him like that."

"Well, I'll tell you this. You show him the door or I'll leave! You choose!"

Carson was stunned at the way Ingrid was handling him. He wasn't about to turn against his cousin for anyone. He walked out of the room and slammed the door behind him.

Trevon was about to nod off on the couch when he saw his cousin pacing the floor.

"What's wrong, man?"

"We need to talk, Cuz."

"What's on your mind?"

"I just want to know one thing, Trevon. Are you taking your medicine?"

Trevon dropped his head and sucked in a deep gulp of air. He looked back at his cousin as a lonely tear ran down his cheek.

"I don't feel like taking so many pills a day. The medicine keeps me tired and slow to respond, like a zombie."

"But, how can you live without it!"

"Don't matter. The disease has spread throughout my body, Carson. It doesn't make any difference whether I take it or not. I don't know how long I have left to live."

"Why are you talking like that? You need to take your medicine, man! It'll help with the pain at least and slow down the process," Carson tried to convince his cousin.

"But Carson, I'm tired of running from my past! I can't sleep at night from reliving the things I've done: Devon's death, beating up my father, the murders in Cali, and hurtin' Crystal and Jonetta.

Carson's eyes perked up at the mention of Crystal. Maybe what Ingrid told him was true after all. It was still hard to believe, even with Trevon standing right in front of him.

"Trevon! You've got strength, Bro! This is no time to give up when you have withstood Aunt Minnie dying, finding out that your father was, but most of all, losing the other half of your soul."

"Yes, and to be honest, I haven't felt complete since Devon's been gone. I felt like when he died, he took a part of me with him."

Carson leaned towards his cousin and wrapped both arms around him. "I'm down with you for life, Cuz, right or wrong."

The Boss Take Over

Early the next morning Trevon awoke to the sound of his cousin and Ingrid in a heated argument. Tired of feeling unwanted, he jumped up off the couch and paced back and forth through the living room, contemplating on his next move. He needed to make amends with Jonetta before it was too late. Trevon grabbed Carson's cell phone off the kitchen counter and stepped out on the balcony. As he keyed in his wife's number, he paused for a moment, thinking of how Jonetta would respond to his pleas. He knew she hated what he'd done to their family, and feared that she, too, might not want anything to do with him. Although he dreaded making the call, Trevon realized that Jonetta was his true heart. He had to find a way to make her forgive him. He pressed the call button and the phone rang twice before a tired-sounding Jonetta picked up.

"Hey, Carson. What's up?"

"This ain't Carson. This is me, Babe."

The line was silent for a minute.

"Trevon, how are you calling me from Carson's phone? Why are you even calling me at all?"

"What do you mean why? I am still your husband!"

"Trevon, listen. In the last year, you've shown me a side of you that I never thought I'd see. You've destroyed what we had single-handedly.

"Jonetta I admit that I've made a few mistakes in my life that I'm not proud of, but you promised me that you would stay down through thick and thin, and now it sounds like you givin' up on me."

"How far down did you want me to go before I finally woke up, Trevon?

"But you don't give up on a man you love, Jonetta! A man that would die from the very thought of someone fucking over you, even if it cost me my own life!"

"Giving up? Trevon, I haven't been in love with you for some time now. You made my heart hard, and left my soul on fire with your perverted ways. I stood by like a fool allowing the man I was in love with to destroy the daughter I always wanted."

"Jonetta," Trevon started, but he realized she'd hung up on him before he could get her name out.

As he turned to go back inside, he saw Ingrid marching towards the door, bags packed. From the look on Carson's face, he realized that he not only destroyed his own marriage, but he had destroyed Carson's, too.

Chapter 15

At first it was easy. Crystal hung out downtown for a while, admiring the people in Sundance Square. There were people in business suits going to meetings, couples holding hands, and a few random people that seemed without purpose, just trying to figure out a way to earn money and eat. That was her problem, now. But while she was sitting in the car waiting for Sam and Jonetta, she decided that starving would be better than going back to the Barnes house with a crazy, abusive father and a mother in denial. She just couldn't take that anymore.

Some of the people downtown was friendly. They smiled and spoke to her, and sometimes they offered her candy, chips, or something to drink, but she had to be careful. She didn't want to jump from "the frying pan into the fire," as Big Mama used to stay. She didn't want to wind up with a pimp like Boss or a pervert like Trevon. So she was careful to stay out of sight as much as possible, and not to look too needy.

She wandered over to the AMC Movie Theater on Third Street, hoping to see someone she knew, a friend from school, maybe, who might treat her to a movie. A hot dog and some popcorn sure would be good about now. She was down to two dollars and change, now. And while the weather had been nice so far during the day, it got cold at night, and finding shelter was a whole 'nother challenge. She paced in front of the theater, pretending to study the movie posters on the building.

A policeman on a bicycle pulled up to the curb. He smiled at her as he parked his bike and started scrolling through his cell phone. A knot formed in her stomach as she started to worry about getting picked up by the cops. But why would they? She hadn't broken any laws and Jonetta certainly wouldn't have reported her as a runaway. She knew the family stayed as far away from the police as possible, so she took a deep breath and walked away.

She'd only been on her own a couple of days. And while she had sometimes been able to get something to eat from strangers, she didn't have a place to sleep or wash up. She thought about going to a shelter. The Salvation Army Night Shelter was within walking distance, but the fear of being reported and sent home put that option off the table.

Hoping for a miracle, she walked around the area looking for a "Now Hiring" sign at one of the restaurants. If she could find some place to work and hang out, and earn tips to get money right away, she could live on her own for a while. She'd never had a job before, but she convinced herself that she could, and would, be willing to do just about anything. She walked up and down several blocks, and even stepped inside and asked some of the managers if they were hiring, but her efforts were fruitless. She hadn't eaten yet today, and it felt like another cold front was moving in.

Back where she started, she stepped inside the lobby of the theater and continued to stare at the posters. The usher taking tickets eyed her suspiciously as she crept closer, trying to sneak in with a crowd of moviegoers. Just as she thought she had made it, the manager approached her and asked her for her ticket stub. All she could do was pretend to look for it unsuccessfully, and then go back outside. The policeman was still there, sitting on his bike. This time, he didn't smile.

"Are you okay, Miss?" he asked politely.

"Yes, I'm fine," Crystal replied. She had no idea which way to go now. The movies had been her best option.

She walked a few blocks and wound upon Main Street in front of Jakes, a "Chili's" type restaurant that served mostly burgers and beer. The smell of fries and grilled onions teased her palate, and she just had to get off her feet. When the server offered to seat her, she accepted, and explained that she was waiting for her boyfriend. She spent thirty minutes browsing through the menu, warding off the waitress every time she asked if she was ready to order. Finally, she ordered a "Jakes' Special" with sweet potato fries, deciding that she was close enough to the door to make a run for it when the server went into the kitchen.

Relieved when the waitress brought her food, she paced herself. She wanted to take her time and relish the first real meal she'd had in twenty-four hours. She wanted to have a reason to stay there as long as possible. She pretended to be embarrassed that her boyfriend never showed up, and the server smiled sympathetically.

When she finished her hamburger and fries, the girl brought the bill and disappeared into the kitchen again. Crystal seized the moment to bolt for the door.

Of course she had to run. The manager might run out of the restaurant and try to chase her down. So she ran and ducked into the first breezeway she saw, hoping no one from the restaurant had tracked her. But just as she ducked in and was catching her breath, the bike cop rolled up in front of her. How would she explain running back there like that?

"Are you sure you're all right, Miss?" he said sternly this time.

"I'm fine. I told you."

"May I see some ID, please?"

"I left my wallet at home," she lied.

"Are you over eighteen? You should carry an ID at all times," the officer continued.

"I know," Crystal stuttered. "I . . . I j-just forgot it."

"I'll need your name and address, Ma'am," he said without taking his eyes off of her. Then he started scrolling through his phone as if he was looking for something.

Crystal's mind was blank. Should she tell the truth and give her real name or should she make up something?

"Crystal," slipped out before thinking it through. "King," she sputtered a few seconds later.

He looked like he didn't believe her. "And your address?"

"What lie to tell now?" she asked herself. She came up with "I live in Meadowbrook."

"I'll need your parent's phone number to verify this."

One lie just led to another. "The phone is out," she said impatiently.

As the officer looked her directly in the eye, he said, "Look, Ma'am. You can either give me a working phone number, even a family member or friend, or I'll have to take you to the station and check out your story."

Crystal's mind failed her again. She couldn't remember anybody's phone number. She'd left her phone at Aunt Ingrid's when Sam forced her into her car.

He signaled a police car over and said something to the driver. Then he opened the door for her to get into the back seat.

"Why are you doing this to me?" she demanded. "I didn't do anything!"

"You've been acting suspiciously all afternoon, wandering the vicinity, going in and out of several businesses. When I saw you run into that breezeway, I thought something might be wrong."

So Crystal had set off the alarm to the cop herself. Maybe she could still get out of it, even though there were two policemen, now.

"Look, Officer. I was supposed to meet my boyfriend at a restaurant and he didn't show up. I didn't want to have to call my mom and ask her to come and get me. She doesn't like him anyway. I'll do anything if you won't take me in. Anything. She'll be so mad."

"What do you mean by that, Ma'am?"

"Whatever it is you wish for! Anything!" Crystal pleaded.

The officers looked at each other and shook their heads. She really hadn't meant it to sound that way. Now she was really in trouble.

"Do you want to add 'propositioning an officer' to the complaint?"

"No, Sir," Crystal sighed as she scooted back in her seat for her first ride in a police car.

As it turned out, the Department of Child Protective Services had reported Crystal as missing. When they were called to the school after the fight with Jonetta, the principal had told her to wait for them in his office, but sensing danger, she had sneaked out and hidden in the auditorium until after school when she thought they'd be gone. That's when Ingrid found her, getting it on with Coach. Between going with Ingrid and getting into the car with Sam, they hadn't had a chance to track her down. The police officer must have identified her by their description, or the school could have handed over her yearbook picture. Either way, she was now in custody.

Crystal was temporarily placed in the Tarrant County Juvenile Detention Center. There, she shared a room with three other girls, runaways and victims of abuse like she was. After sharing their stories, she decided to come clean about what Trevon had done to her. Anything was better than going back there.

In the following weeks, Crystal was drilled almost daily about her life with Jonetta and Trevon. Rather than take a chance on being sent back to them, she told Pamela Burnette, her counselor, every sick detail.

During the first few visits, the teen was emotionally withdrawn. She said very little in her sessions for fear of being judged, but eventually she loosened up and told the entire story to her counselor, from how ugly she felt when Trevon first started groping her breasts and feeling between her legs, to his demanding that she suck his penis and let him go inside her. She even told her about Boss, and the horrible things he had done to her, from making her wear a dog collar to the beatings, starving, and isolation.

The woman could not hold back her own tears as Crystal described Trevon's actions and how Jonetta just stood by as if she didn't know. Miss Burnette convinced her to tell the police so that he would no longer be a threat to her. As far as Crystal knew, he was still at the mental hospital, but he could get out of there at any time. If he was in jail, he couldn't find her and force his crazy self on her again. She would not have to live the rest of her life looking over her shoulder.

Crystal could have told them about what happened in California, too, but she didn't. Despite how Trevon treated her when he started to change, he was the one who had insisted on coming to California and rescuing her from Boss and Paulette. And for that she was grateful. If they hadn't come for her, she surely would be dead by now. So somehow, all that family loyalty that Sam talked about had made an impact, and she didn't want to drag her, Ingrid, and Carson into it, especially not Ingrid. She wasn't even there.

And Ingrid was the one person she had felt she could trust. But when she told her about Trevon abusing her, Ingrid didn't believe her. She seemed to at first, but all it took was a little coaxing from Sam and Ingrid assumed she was lying, too. She tried to send her back to Jonetta, so to hell with all of them.

The girls were schooled right there at the center. No more Alexander Hamilton Prep. She missed a few friends, mostly guys, but she was so humiliated that last day that she didn't care if she never went back there again. She hoped she could go back home to Big Mama and maybe finish high school at the Heights, but she just didn't know if they would let her go. So she tried to be on her best behavior, follow the directions of the teachers and counselors, and devote her time to her school work.

One of the routine procedures for admitting a child to CPS was a thorough physical exam. Since she was hardly ever sick and Jonetta didn't want anyone to examine her, Crystal was never taken to the doctor. She didn't need it, Jonetta told her. But when the lab tests came back, the doctor had to break some devastating news to Crystal. She was HIV positive.

Crystal had just begun to be whole again, to show signs of real progress. She sensed something was wrong when the counselor made an appointment for a conference with the doctor. But since she felt fine, she thought this was just part of the routine. When the doctor said, "You're HIV positive," Crystal blocked everything else out. She couldn't believe her ears. She sat there, stunned, without moving. Then she asked him to repeat what he said.

"You're HIV positive, Crystal. I'm sorry."
Then she cried, "Noooo! Noooo!" as she fell down to her knees. Her life was just beginning again, and now this!

"Why?" she cried. "Why me? I'm never gonna be free of him. Never!"
The doctor looked on sympathetically, trying to think of a way to console her, but he was at a loss for words. He closed the door to his office and called for Miss Burnette.

Miss Burnette explained that being HIV positive wasn't the death sentence that it used to be, that while there still wasn't a cure, with the right medication, she could still have a normal life. She brought up the example of Magic Johnson and his wife, Cookie.

Crystal just sat there, staring out into space. But the counselor stayed with her until she was ready to leave the office. She knew Crystal would have no privacy in her room, and she needed to cry, to release her feelings in some way. So she took her back to her own office and let her lie down on the couch. That couch became Crystal's refuge over the next few weeks. It was the only place she felt she didn't have to hide her condition.

It was on that couch that Crystal confessed to the feeling of dread she'd had lately, waiting for something terrible to happen. She had thought her fears were based on Trevon coming after her. She had thought that problem would be solved once he was in police custody, and Miss Burnette assured him he would be. He came after her, alright. He'd be with her for the rest of her life. With that piece of news, Crystal just wanted to die.

After several weeks, Crystal and the counselor became very close. Miss Burnette became more of a mentor; nurturing Crystal back to the carefree girl she once was as she worked towards graduation. She showed Crystal how to break the cycle of depression and transition her mind to a higher level of thinking. Crystal realized that part of her loneliness and her desire to please men came from the fact that she never had the opportunity to get to know her mother. Neither Big Mama nor Jonetta had been able to fill that void.

She sat in awe as her mentor went off the record and explained the source of her mission. Miss Burnette had been a battered teen whose mother had been killed when she was very young. She was a victim of sexual abuse by her stepfather. Things got so bad that she tried to kill herself. She truly understood how Crystal felt.

"It's amazing how you went through almost the exact same experiences that I did and you were able to come out just fine, above your circumstances. You sowed your own seeds, enough to see sunlight through the cracks in the concrete, and you didn't even have a mentor. You are truly my hero, Miss Burnette. I don't know where I would be now if it weren't for you."

"I am so glad to be able to help you pick up the pieces of your life, Crystal. It makes me feel like the degree was well worth my time working for it."

"It's worth it, all right. I know I'm not the only person you've helped like this. I hope someday I can do the same for someone else."

"You can. All you have to do is stay focused, work hard, and complete your education. And speaking of education, I have some good news. You'll be returning to your grandmother's home and you can get your diploma from your old high school. How do you feel about that?

"For real?" She yelled as she hugged the counselor. "Really? When can I go?

"As soon as the paperwork is approved. I wanted to check with you before proceeding any further."

"Well, proceed on, Miss Burnette! I can't wait to get back to my life before all this stuff happened. I can't wait to go back with my Big Mama!"

"I really hope this is the first of many good things happening for you, Crystal. I'll do everything I can to make this happen as soon as possible."

"You just don't know, Miss Burnette. This is the best news I've had in a long time. This means I can graduate with my class next month. Will you come see me walk across the stage?"

"I will definitely be there to see my young sister begin her new life."

"I am so thankful for you and the things you have taught me both in and out of the counseling sessions."

"Look, you keep your head to the sky, get that diploma and let's set out across the Metropolis inspiring young women to overcome obstacles like you have. We can use your testimony as a platform for success. I volunteer with a nonprofit organization that motivates young people to follow their dreams.

"What could I possibly say? I'm just getting started on my own journey."

"That's just it. You've started on your journey despite all the terrible things that have happened to you."

"But won't people look down on me for what I've done? If they know I'm HIV positive, they won't want to come near me!

"Listen. You didn't have a choice in any of that. You'd be surprised how many girls have had similar experiences. Once you see how many young women you are able to influence, you will feel proud of yourself, and then that dead weight will be lifted from your shoulders."

"If it can lift this weight from me, I'm definitely in." Crystal said, grinning from ear to ear.

Chapter 16

Jonetta sat up, back slumped against the headboard. She was angry at Trevon for leaving the facility when he knew he was a sick man. She realized he'd be trying to come by as soon as he felt the coast was clear. She was afraid of how he'd react when she rejected him. She decided to call her sister for support. Jonetta leaned over and grabbed her phone off the nightstand. She pressed the call button on "Bad Bitch," and the phone rang once.

"Hello," Sam picked up.

"Damn! I see you still ain't got no man tapping that ass these days!"

"Look, I wouldn't give a damn if a man was full-stride camel style inside of me. When you call, I'm gon' answer the phone regardless. Anyway, what's up?

"Girl, Trevon called talking crazy, got me worked-up. 'Talkin' bout he wants to see me!"

"Okay then, send his ass a picture and let him paste it to his wall in his room," Sam joked.

"He's out!"

"What? How the hell did he get out?"

"Shit! I don't know! I told him I didn't want to see him, but I know he's not gonna take no for an answer."

"What time is it?" Sam demanded.

"It's almost midnight. I'm sorry to call you so late."

"Don't even worry about it," Sam replied. Sensing the fear in her sister's voice, she decided she'd spend a couple of nights with Jonetta.

"Take a ten count, Sister. I'm on my way."

"Oh, thank you, Sam! Thank you so much!"

Sam threw some clothes in a suitcase, grabbed her flask and her piece, and headed out the door.

When she pulled on to Jonetta's street, she looked around at every car sitting still; making sure that Trevon wasn't somehow already stalking the house. Sam called Jonetta's and asked her to raise the garage. She pulled in and Jonetta quickly shut it down behind her.

"Damn! Who in the hell is this texting me at this time of night?" Sam went to the screen to check the text and was shocked by the ominous message, in all caps. "YOU AND THAT BITCH ASS JONETTA, SOME DEAD HOES."

Jonetta stood in the doorway waiting for her sister. When she spotted the faraway look on Sam's face, the pit of her stomach gave off an eerie feeling that something was terribly wrong.

"What's wrong, Sis? Why you looking like that?"

Sam couldn't believe her eyes. She was furious at the threatening text, but at the same time she was nervous, wondering who in the hell would send that message. She sat quietly, her mind racing through her past.

"Sam!"

She snapped out of the daze and looked up at Jonetta. "Yeah?"

"What's the problem? Why you sitting stuck like that?

Sam grabbed her bag from the back seat and went inside the house without saying a word. She set the suitcase down in the kitchen and gave Jonetta a hug.

"I'm here, Jonetta. No more worries."

"Sam, I know when something's going on with you because you have this faraway look in your eyes. What's going on?"

Sam showed Jonetta the text message and she, too, stared at the bold letters as she reflected on her past. Within seconds, Jonetta came to a conclusion.

"It's him, Sam. I told you he called earlier."

Sam stood, wondering if Trevon had seen her pull into the garage, and then sent the threatening message. But she quickly realized it wasn't like Trevon to send messages through phone texts or calls. When he turned into Li'l Daddy and came at you, you got the message straight up.

"Nah, Jojo, this didn't come from Trevon. He wouldn't send a message like this. This is from some hater."

Jonetta opened the cabinet and pulled out a bottle of Hennessy.

"Girl, I know it's late, but I need me a drink. You want one?"

"Pour me a double shot of that shit." Sam responded.

Jonetta fixed herself and Sam a drink, all the while peeping out the kitchen window for any sign of Trevon.

"Here." Jonetta said as she set the drink down on the table in front of Sam. But there would be no sipping for Sam. She raised the glass up high as if she was making a toast, and then turned it up to her mouth, consuming every drop.

"Now I'm ready to handle my mutha fuckin' business if he comes through with that bullshit. Where is that gun you said you had to hide from him when he was acting crazy?"
"Oh, I got a few pistols I found of his, after many nights of him acting a damn fool. Come on in here."
Jonetta led Sam through the hallway and stopped just below the attic door. She stood on her tip-toes and tugged at the cord until the steps came down.

"I put 'em in the attic. There should be a forty-five and two smaller guns under the insulation."
Jonetta climbed up the steps and retrieved all three weapons.

"Damn! This big mutha fucka here oughta' blow a hole right through his ass." Sam said, as she held the large caliber weapon away from her.

They both returned to the living room and Sam put the guns on the coffee table.

"What's really going on, Jo?"
"Sam, it's so much."
"Well, start at the beginning. 'Cause' I ain't got nothing but time."
Jonetta took a long swallow of her whiskey and took a deep breath.

"It all kicked off right after we got back from California. He started tossing and turning in his sleep. He would get up in the middle of the night chanting Devianna's name over and over, hands spread wide like he was praying to the ceiling. Then one night I noticed he added Crystal's name to the chant. So I crept around for the next few nights watching his every movement. When I caught his perverted ass with my daughter between his legs, I wanted to blow his head off right then. But something in me wouldn't let me pull the trigger."

"I don't know why the hell not!" Sam responded.

"I know. I know. But I didn't. I stood by like a damn fool and watched as he violated what youth Crystal still had left in her."
Visibly upset, Sam demanded, "Was his sick ass fucking on her?"

"I caught him a couple times on top of her," she confessed as she broke down in tears.

"I can't believe you, Jonetta. You, of all people, let him do that?"

"I can't believe me, either, Sam. I was stupid in love, so blind that I put my hands over my own eyes to hide from the truth." Jonetta responded as she covered her mouth to cough.

Sam stared at her, realizing that she was not herself. "Jonetta, have you been taking your medicine?"

"I do on some days, and then on others, I just stay in the bed all day."

"You gotta take your medicine, Jonetta, before you end up in the hospital."

"Yeah, I know." Jonetta continued. "Trevon got worse and worse over the next few months. He stopped taking his meds and he had terrible mood swings and depression. I just kept hoping he would get better. But he didn't. That's why I had to have him committed."

Sam nodded, patting Jonetta's hand as she remembered the dinner when she'd told everyone about Trevon's illness as well as her own.

Jonetta coughed again.

Sam looked at her dwindling body and couldn't believe she had missed the signs herself. Jonetta was really sick.

"That day you picked me up from jail," Jonetta continued, "was the worst day of my life. We had just got back from seeing Trevon at Patton's. He was acting crazy then, remember? Huggin' us one minute and cussin' us out the next!"

"Yeah, I thought I was gonna have to beat his ass out there!" Sam said.

When I got home," Jonetta added, I got a call from Patton's saying Trevon tried to kill himself."

Sam gasped. "What?" she charged. She had no idea about this.

"They had to sedate him and told me to just wait until the next day to drive back out there 'cause he'd be sleep."

"Did they know what caused it?" Sam interrupted.

"Same thing they always said. He was bipolar or something like that."

"Bipolar? That's just somethin' doctors make up to explain why people act stupid!'"

Jonetta laughed weakly. "Maybe so. But then I listened to the next voicemail and it was Crystal's counselor calling to say she'd been skippin' classes. She was getting' wild and I went up to the school. I hit her in front of the principal. That's how I wound up in jail."

Sam nodded, remembering the details of that day.

"Then when you picked me up, that's when Crystal disappeared."

Sam recalled the afternoon she left Crystal in the Benz while she met the bondsman and when they got back to the car, Crystal was gone.

All they knew was Crystal was picked up by CPS, and they never saw her again. Jonetta hadn't even told Sam that when she tried to get her back, she was told that would be impossible. Crystal didn't want to come home. The case was being investigated. No telling what Sam might have done if she knew that Crystal had talked to the police. That was one thing Sam wouldn't stand for, going against family.

"Girl, why didn't you tell me what was going on? You really been going through some shit and I was so caught up with my own drama with men that I didn't even recognize! Why didn't you tell me all this before?" she yelled.

Tears were streaming down Jonetta's face as Sam reached over and hugged her sister. They all used to be so close and so happy.   '

"Where did it all go wrong?" thought Sam.

Jonetta got up to get a box of tissue and just as she placed it on the table, Sam's signature ring went off.

Silence fell over the room when the phone rang. Both women sat staring in the direction of Sam's cell phone, until Sam leaned forward to check the caller I. D. There was no number on the screen.

"Somebody's calling private."

"Yeah, that's probably him right there." Jonetta nervously replied.

"Hello!" Sam barked into the phone.

"What up, Bitches!"

"Who the hell is this playing on my phone?

"Bitch, you know who this is. And this ain't no game. It's the same mutha fucka that left that text message. Since Trevon's child molesting ass is on lock down, I got plenty of time to get at him. I'm gon' get you hoes first."

Sam couldn't believe she was hearing a voice from the dead. The caller sounded like Paulette James, but she wasn't sure. She rushed over to the kitchen window and looked out into the driveway, all while holding the phone intently listening to the woman's voice.

"What yo' nervous ass looking around for? I got both of you mutha fuckas on the scope right now. But I'd rather see the fear in your eyes up close and personal when you take your last breath. That's the only reason I ain't blew your fuckin' head off yet. And don't worry about Crystal. She's with real family now. Not somewhere suckin' on Trevon's dirty ass dick."

Sam wanted to respond, but she wasn't sure what to say. Paulette was supposed to be left for dead.

"Oh, yeah! Keep your eyes wide open 'cause it's on and poppin' until I'm dead for sho'!"

The look on Sam's face told Jonetta that she knew the caller. Her face paled to a lighter shade as if she had seen a ghost. In fact, she had heard one.

Jonetta walked up beside her and planted her ear to the back of the phone. Sam turned to her and whispered the word "Paulette," as Jonetta's mouth dropped in shock.

"That can't be! We killed her in California! You did it yourself, Sam, with that black tar heroin you scored! Carson got rid of the body!" Jonetta was hysterical now.

"I know! I know! But somethin' must have happened 'cause that sho' was her! Damn! How'd she get back here?"

"No! No!" Jonetta screamed. Lately, she believed all her bad luck was God punishing her for not protecting Crystal. She slid off the couch and started rolling back and forth on the floor.

"I'm so sorry, Crystal!" So sorry!"

Sam knew she had to get Jonetta under control. Between Paulette's threats and Trevon's craziness, they had to be on point. They had to be ready for anything. It was going to be a long night!

Sam went to the bedroom to look for Jonetta's meds. Maybe she could identify something that would calm her down. She brought the bag out to the living room so she could read the labels and keep an eye on Jonetta.

Trevon stood looking at the back of his cousin's head, as Carson walked off into the bedroom and shut the door behind him. He was at his wit's end with destroying the lives before him. After a few minutes, Trevon knocked on the bedroom door.

"Yeah! Carson yelled out.

"Hey, Cuz, can you give me a few dollars. I'm going to walk down to the store and get me a beer or somethin' to calm my nerves."

Carson opened the door and handed Trevon a twenty dollar bill.

"You want anything?"

"Naw, I'm cool. You just be careful man. Remember, you're not a free man."

"I'm good."

Trevon walked out of the apartment rapping, "It's just me against the world, Baby." He knew Ingrid didn't care much for him and his cousin. And although he said he was down for life, Carson sure seemed to be taking Ingrid's leaving pretty hard. He walked across the main street to the store and grabbed two forty ounces of Old English malt liquor. As he walked towards the counter to pay for them, Trevon ran into an older man that he recognized from the projects.

"Hey, man, what's going on?" Trevon asked.

The man paused for a minute as he tried to put a name with the face.

"This Li'l Daddy, man."

"Li'l Daddy! Li'l Daddy from the Como projects?"

"Yeah, man. It's me. I been sick for a few weeks and lost a little weight."

"You lost a lot of weight, my man, I didn't even recognize you. What you been up to?

"Just chillin' and staying out the way."

"That's a good thing."

"Which way are you going?

"I'm headed home man. I just got off work and I'm tired."

"Can I pay you to drop me off?
"Where?"
"Over on Bryant Irving Road."
"Sure, man. Come on. No charge."

Trevon jumped in the passenger seat and cracked the top on his forty ounce. He offered the man a drink but he declined. By the time they reached Bryant Irving Road, he had finished one bottle and was half-way through the other.

"You can drop me off at the next corner, man. I stay just up the road here," Trevon said, pointing up at the ritzy homes.

The old man looked at where Trevon was pointing and frowned. He wondered if he was dropping his old friend off to burglarize a house in the neighborhood. He sure didn't look like he lived there. So once the car door was shut, he pulled off in a hurry, not wanting any part of what the man was about to do.

Trevon took off and walked two blocks, sweating profusely, looking over his shoulder every step of the way. The malt liquor had him swimming in a sea of guilt. He decided to try to call on the Lord before he made it to Jonetta. He needed all the help he could get.

"Lord, it's me, Trevon. Can you hear me? I'm in trouble again, Lord, and I'm asking for help. I've lost just about everything . . . my twin, his baby, my daughter, and my wife. When I didn't hear back from you all those times before, I just gave up. It's hard to believe in something I can't see.

But everything's going from bad to worse. This AIDS is eatin' away at me. I have been locked up with crazy people. And the only person who really loved me has given up on me, too. I've mistreated my child. I've cost my cousin his marriage. I just need one more chance to prove to Jonetta how much I love her. I didn't mean all those bad things I did. Or what I said. Please, God! Help me get her back!

"Lord, can you hear me? Are you there? Are you real?"

With the silence, Trevon broke down on the ground in tears.

Sam rummaged through the bag of meds. She found several bottles full of AZT and Topamax that had never been opened. Looking at the dates on the labels, she could only conclude that Jonetta hadn't been taking her meds for a month or more. Maybe they were Trevon's, and he was taking his meds at the hospital. That would explain the unopened prescriptions. No, she told herself. That would be too easy. Jonetta had admitted as much to her. She had given up on life, and was trying to speed up the process.

She glanced over at Jonetta and patted her cheek. "Come on, Jonetta! Pull yourself together! Calm down. What can you take here?"

Jonetta just shook her head from side to side. She was convinced that either Trevon or Paulette was coming to kill her, and she felt that she deserved it.

"Well, you might be ready to die, but I'm not!" Sam told her. But her words fell on deaf ears. Jonetta was shaking and crying, totally out of control. Sam rummaged through the bag again and found a label she knew . . . valium. 'Maybe this would calm her down'.

Sam ran to the kitchen to get a bottle of water, and then shook two pills out of the valium container. She pulled Jonetta half way up from the floor and leaned her against the couch. Then she tilted her head back, placed one pill on her tongue, and tried to get Jonetta to swallow some water behind it.

She started gagging and choking, spitting the water out. And then a round of coughing came thundering out of her mouth. Sam was afraid she would puncture a lung, she was coughing so hard. She tried slapping her on the back. The coughing subsided.

Jonetta just kept rolling her head from side to side against the couch, mumbling, "No! No!" over and over again. Her voice was getting softer. Maybe she would drift on off to sleep, Sam thought. Maybe it's good that she couldn't get those pills down.

"Poor thing. How much could one human being take?" Sam asked herself. She reached over and grabbed the Hennessy from the coffee table and took a swig straight from the bottle. It burned slightly as it went down, then a feeling of calm washed over her. She took a bigger gulp and got up to check the lock on the front door. As she moved back towards the couch, she saw a tiny red dot on the wall facing the window. She knew exactly what that meant. Growing up in the projects had provided her with an education about the dangers of the streets, and she knew a red dot from the sight of a gun when she saw one.

Her gun was ready for action in her purse. The ones Jonetta brought out were on the table next to the Hennessy. She had to go towards the wall to move Jonetta away from the path of the red dot sight and to grab one of the guns. She could see the sight moving along the wall above the couch.

Sam got down on her knees and crawled along the floor towards Jonetta, still moaning but unable to move. "Jonetta!" she called out.

There was still no response. She grabbed her legs and pulled her towards her, away from the couch. Then she reached up to pick up the forty-five.

Pop! The shot hit the wall, shattering both the window and the mirror behind the couch.

A knot formed in Sam's stomach but it did not deter her from planning an escape or protecting them both. She released the safety on the gun and cocked it, ready for action.

The raspy sound of Paulette's voice yelled from the street. "You ready to die, Bitch? If you ain't, you betta get ready!"

"Come on! You think you bad enough? I 'killed' you once and I'll do it again! This time, you won't go so easy! I'm the baddest bitch on this block!"

Sam leaned towards the opening where the window had been and took aim at the darkness. She didn't know if there was a full round in Trevon's gun so she had to choose her shots carefully. She couldn't afford to miss or to run out of bullets. She fired off her first shot. There was no sound after the bullet left the chamber.

"Fuck that!" Paulette responded. "Like I told you, I want to see your fuckin' face when you die, just like you did me. But the difference is you won't be comin' back!"

"Then you betta git yo' ass on in here," Sam yelled back. "Cause I ain't goin' nowhere!" She cocked her gun again. She could hear Jonetta moaning on the floor still, trying to get up off the floor.

As Sam moved to push her down again, she heard a rush toward the house.

"Get down, Jonetta!" Sam screamed. She lunged toward Jonetta to keep her from getting in the path of the red light. As they both tumbled to the floor, Sam heard another pop. This time it was closer. The shooter had moved to the edge of the yard, it seemed. The lamp on the end table was now in pieces on the floor.

Sam heard the sound of the garage door opening. Nobody could get in without knowing the combination. Paulette had found out a lot about them since she'd been back, but she couldn't have gotten the security code to the garage. No way. It must be Trevon, she figured, coming to claim his woman. She didn't have time to worry about him now.

Suddenly, a heavy figure hurdled towards her and Sam fired again, hoping to hit her point blank. Evidently she missed, because the figure kept advancing closer. A final shot rang through the darkness and Trevon screamed, "Jonetta!" as he fell dead in front of the busted window. He was hit from the back and the bullet ripped through his organs, blowing out his chest completely.

The red dot vanished along with Paulette as sirens converged on the house.

Chapter 17

Samantha woke up with the sun on most days, but this day it was harder than usual. She squint her eyes and looked over at the clock by her bed. The numbers told her it was 9:15, but it felt more like six A.M. Did she have too much to drink last night? Last night. Then it dawned on her. Last night she stopped by the Dew Drop Inn on the way home from the hospital.

Jonetta was admitted after Trevon was killed. She was already sick from not taking her meds and she just fell apart when she heard Trevon call out her name just before the fatal shot. The police had rushed in and called the ambulance. They'd been looking for him for those sexual abuse charges, and they knew he had escaped from Patton's. The gunshots must have triggered them to come right away. Sam figured Crystal must have told them everything. Carson showed up when they were taking the body out, too late to save him this time. He cried like a baby when he realized that Trevon was gone. He had been like a brother since Big Twin died. Like a sister, Sam had gone to the hospital every day since then. There's nothing like family.

She still couldn't believe the events of a week ago, when that crazy ass Paulette came around looking for her with blood on her mind. It was bad enough that the bitch she thought she had killed in Cali had come back to haunt her, but she had the nerve to try to hunt her down in some stupid revenge move. It's a good thing game recognize game, and she was no fool. But she couldn't believe it was Trevon that saved their lives. Trevon, of all people. He went through a lot of changes lately, with the AIDS, the hospital, and that stuff about Crystal, but deep down, he was a good man and a true friend to the end. If it weren't for Trevon, both she and Jonetta would be dead for sure. No matter what anybody said, Trevon was all right with her.

A chill ran down her spine at the thought of it, and she threw back the covers and headed to the kitchen. She didn't want to re-imagine the events of that night. So she filled the pot with water, dipped out three scoops of coffee, put them in the top of the coffee pot, and pressed "On."

A few minutes later, she sat down at the breakfast bar sipping her "cup a Joe," as Mama Dee used to call it. She thought about Mama Dee most times when she was drinking coffee at home like this. Mama Dee loved her coffee as much as she loved her booze. Sam loved them both, too.

She reached inside the cabinet for the party-sized bottle of Hennessy to top off her coffee. She felt the edges of a headache creeping in, and the best way to fight a hangover or a headache was to fight fire with fire. So she poured a double shot into her coffee, stirred it with her finger, and took a sip. Between the warmth of the brew and the heat of the whiskey, she felt renewed. As she started her second cup of the tainted lava, tears began to well up in her eyes. Sometimes without warning, she felt Mama Dee all around her, but she couldn't see her unless she pulled out that old scrapbook, filled with memories of her childhood and lost youth.

Even though she was alone, she quickly wiped the tears away for fear that someone would see her crying and perceive it as weak. Sam was a soldier and timid moments were never meant to be part of her program. She walked over to the couch and reached under the coffee table for the old photo album Mama Dee left behind. She opened it to the first page and read the caption:

To whoever may be looking through these pictures, it's approximately six generations of handsome hustlers enclosed in this photo album. Be careful how you handle it.
Yours truly,
Double OG, Mama Dee.

P.S. The one and only.
If there's another, she must be a phony.

Sam shook her head and smiled. She knew Mama Dee

wouldn't compromise her words for anybody. She flipped through the pages, pausing on a childhood picture of Jonetta, Cynthia, Ingrid, herself and Paulette at one of Big Kenny's many barbecues he blessed the "Jets" with before being sentenced to life. She stared at the picture close enough to spot Paulette's older sister Barbara in the background and chuckled out loud thinking of the day Big Kenny and the GNB rolled through every street in the projects tossing out wads of cash. Barbara was so loyal she went up every street checking people about picking up Kenny's lost cash. Those were the good old days. What had happened to them? She could hear Mama Dee's words just as clearly as if she was standing right there. "We all got older," she'd say, when anybody asked her why she stopped gang-banging.

 In the last few years, Sam had lost a many soldiers to the game, either through the eyes of the undertaker or to the system, with a basketball score as their sentence to be served out. She couldn't believe that everyone in her once tight-knit circle was either dead or doing their own thing. Her sister was gravely ill. The AIDS, accompanied with the depression, had caused Jonetta's health to deteriorate. She knew Ingrid wanted no parts of the street life. She had stuck to her guns. She was so in a forward motion with her life that she had cut Carson loose. When they did get together, Ingrid never wanted to hear about anybody from the "Jets."

At that moment, Sam remembered that today was her birthday. She was thirty years old today. With all the excitement about Trevon and Paulette, she had forgotten all about it. Though she knew it was coming, she couldn't believe it was already here. There's a difference in how people, especially men, see a woman who's twenty-something and how they see one who's in her thirties. Twenty says young and sexy, which she was, without a doubt. Thirty is creeping up on forty, which is middle aged. Sam wondered if she could just get back into bed and turn back the clock. She continued to sip on her special brew as she took stock of her life. She had a beautiful house and plenty of money, most recently from Leon, who had just come through with her share from Ernie's court case. She still couldn't believe a lawyer with a rep like his would throw a case in court. But hey, money talks! She was just glad she got some of it, fifty grand as a matter of fact. Too bad things didn't work out with her and Leon.

She picked and chose her lovers carefully and knew how to get it as well as give it up. But since Leon had left her (and she would only admit that to herself), she realized that as fine as she was and as sexy as she was, she really didn't have anybody special in her life. And she missed that. She liked pleasing a man. Sam had never been one to do without, and while there were always a few prospects at her favorite hot spots, she was beginning to want more. She thought she might have had it with Leon, but he had to go acting a fool and tried to rip her off. So here she was, on her thirtieth birthday, with no one.

Then she tried to push the memory out of her mind. The baby. She had been pregnant once with Big Twin's baby, streets and the next thing she knew, he was demanding that she get an abortion. She had let on like it was no big deal, but it really hurt her. And hurt was something Samantha Williams never allowed the world to see. She and Big Twin had drifted apart after that. She figured he would understand how she felt, but he didn't. So she didn't even tell him that the doctor told her she couldn't have any more children. She didn't tell anyone. Not even her sisters. She figured a man that wanted to do more than "hit it and quit it" wouldn't want her after that, and the family would just feel sorry for her. And if there's one thing neither she nor Mama Dee could stand, it was pity. Then they both moved on. It bothered her when Devon hooked up with Cynthia, but she'd had other men, too, so what could she say? The Double Dutch Queen had been her girl since childhood, so she just played it off and kept on moving. That was the image she put out to the world: Samantha Williams, woman on the move.

But she knew deep down that the reason she risked her life and was even willing to kill, was to save Devon and Cynthia's baby. They got caught up in the drama of saving Crystal after Cynthia died, but Sam never forgot about the baby. One day, she didn't know when or how, but one day, she'd find Devianna.

Meanwhile, "Happy birthday to me," Sam said to herself as she finished her third cup of coffee. Just as she was putting her mug in the sink, her phone rang.

She walked back into her bedroom to get it, and answered on the way back to the kitchen. She was already in a better mood. Hennessey works miracles.

"Yo' dime, yo' time!" she answered playfully.

"Hey, girl! Happy birthday! I bet you thought I forgot."

"Ingrid! It's been a minute. How are you doing?"

"I'm okay. I'm hangin' in there."

"I heard about you and Carson. I'm sorry to hear ya'll broke up. I thought if anybody could make it, you two would."

"I know, right? He just kept making choices I couldn't support. I've been to prison before, and I'm never going back. I worked hard to become a nurse and I'm not throwing that away for anybody. I just had to tell him, if you wanna be a thug, you have to do it without me. Messin' around with Trevon was gonna take him back to jail or to his grave."

"I feel ya, sistuh. I still can't believe all that shit that happened last week. Paulette had come back from the dead trying to kill us, and Trevon steppin' in. That shit was crazy. Like somethin' in a movie!'

"You got that right! But anyhoo, enough of that. I called to see what you wanna do for yo' birthday? I just got off work. I checked on Jonetta before I left. She was sleeping, so I didn't wake her up. I can't believe how much weight she's lost."

"Me, either. That AIDS is killing her. After Crystal ran away, she just started' apart. I don't know whether it was because she missed her so much or because she felt guilty about not protecting her from Trevon, but she got depressed, stopped taking her meds, and just started givin' up on life."

"This is all so sad," Ingrid replied.

"I know. And Trevon escaping from the institution didn't help either. She acted like she was scared of him. He took her through so many changes. I couldn't blame her for not wanting him back, but we'd a both been dead if he hadn't taken that bullet."

'I know. Jonetta couldn't even get out of the hospital to go to the funeral,"

"Just thinkin' about it makes me sad, and I don't wanna be sad today!"

"Well, let's talk about something else. We can go by and see Jonetta later on, if you want. But first, let's go celebrate your birthday!"

"I know what I wanna do first! Let's go to spa, out by Ridgmar Mall! We can do nails and feet, get massages and wraps. The works! It's all on me!"

"Well, all right, then! I could use a good massage for real after the night I had at the hospital. Those chairs are not comfortable."

"I'll pick you up at noon. That's when my favorite masseur checks in. His name is Jerry. And girl, he is fo-ine!" Talk about magic hands!

Ingrid laughed over the phone. "You ain't never gonna change, Sis."

"Why should I?" Sam replied. "You can't improve on perfection!"

It was just like old times except Jonetta wasn't there. Sam and Ingrid had a glorious day at Spa Baby. Jerry, Mr. Magic Hands himself, took care of both of them and he was just as fine as Samantha promised. They got massages and wraps, they did the steam room, and they got mani-pedis. They spent an hour at Macy's. Then they went to Buttons for lunch and lingered over until Happy Hour started.

When the server brought their meals, Ingrid bowed to say grace. She noticed Sam waiting for her to finish with one eye open.

"Sam, you don't bless your food before you eat?"

"Listen. I lost all regard to believing in God when He took Mama from us. I felt like He left us all alone to fend for ourselves."

"But Sam, we were already seasoned and grown enough to stand on our own two feet."

"I know, but I cried and asked Him that day to spare Mama's life, and a week later, we buried her."

"How many times have you asked for something and even promised to deliver something in return and never came through? Be honest, Sam.

"Everybody has done that at some point in time, I'm sure."

"But you're not judged according to their beliefs, Sam. It's what you believe in your heart."

"Okay, Ingrid. Stop preaching. We're finished with this conversation." Sam said as she dug into her chicken wings.

"Sam, if you had a mind, you'd be dangerous."

"I'm dangerous without a mind. What are you talking about?"

"That's exactly what I'm talking about. You don't have a clue.

Ingrid reached for a piece of garlic bread. "By the way, what's happening in the federal case with the Ernie Black and his crew?" Ingrid asked. He was the reason they were all sent to jail except

Sam. Ingrid had never forgiven him.

"Girl, Didn't I tell you?" They charged Ernie as the King Pin and he got life. The rest of them ended up with twenties and thirties, and the snitch only got two years' suspended sentence."

"Man! They really got messed over. What happened?"

"Once they allowed the informant to get on the stand, they didn't have a chance."

"He told everything?"

"Shit. Leon said the man started talking and wouldn't stop until the judge asked him to."

"Did you go to the trial?"

"No. I hate to see somebody go down in court that I once fucked, so I stayed away."

"Sam! You still a potty mouth! Ain't you never gonna change?"

"No, like I told you this morning, you can't improve on perfection."

"Sam, you're still a fool!" Ingrid said chuckling.

As Samantha finished her third "Stevie Wonder" concoction, her cell phone rang.

"Hello, Beautiful. Happy Birthday," said a smooth voice over the phone.

"Leon?"

"Yeah, Baby. It's me. I just wanted you to know I was thinking about you. And I didn't forget your birthday."

"Well, thank you," Sam purred. "It's nice to know you remembered."

"Oh, you are one unforgettable woman, Samantha. What are you doing to celebrate?"

"Me and Ingrid are hanging out. We had a girls' day. Just shopping and spa stuff."

"Well, that's good. So what are your plans for the evening?"

"We were just talking about that. We may go by the hospital and see Jonetta, but we hadn't decided on anything after that."

"I heard about Jonetta and Trevon. I'm so sorry. How is she holding up?"

"You know. Some days are better than others."

"Well, give her my regards when you talk to her. I was hoping to see you tonight."

"Really?" Samantha's ears perked up. She was surprised that Leon was still interested. She thought he had washed his hands of her.

"You're an irresistible woman, Sam. A man could never forget about you."

When Sam's caramel-colored skin turned a deep pink, Ingrid got the hint. She leaned over and tapped Sam on the arm.

"Excuse me a minute, Leon."

She covered the phone as Ingrid leaned in.

"Why don't you go on out with Leon? We've been together all day. I'll go by and visit Jonetta, and then I'm going home to get some sleep."

"You sure?" Sam asked.

"Yeah, girl. Go on out and get yo' freak on. It's been a minute, I know."

"Yes, it has," Sam sighed.

Sam turned back to her phone call. "Okay, Leon. What do you have in mind?"

"Why don't you just dress up like you do, pretty lady? And I'll pick you up at eight."

Sam was grinning from ear to ear. "That would be just fine," she answered, as she sipped the last of her drink and motioned for the check.

A few hours later, Sam sat across from Leon at Abuelos. This was new for them. Before, they had "date nights" at her place or his, or they vacationed out of town. He didn't introduce her to his friends or his co-workers or take her to public events. It was almost as if he was ashamed of her. But this new Leon was sexy and attentive, almost as if he could sense her emotions. He not only pulled out her chair and opened doors for her; he talked about a serious future together. He had never brought up marriage before, but Leon admitted that he was in love with her and wanted to take their relationship to the next level.

Sam was tired of living the single and free life. She understood now that even gigolos got lonely. Dealing with the brothers that wanted no commitment at all was a waste of her precious years. She was now thirty and she wanted a chance at love. Even behind the mask of being a strong woman, Sam wanted someone to call her own.

Although it was hard for Sam to admit, Leon really hurt her when he walked out. Deep down, she really loved Leon, but she would be the last one to admit it.

A week after their reunion date, Sam sat in her living room watching a movie on Lifetime when she heard a vibrating noise coming from her room. She hurried to get her phone and realized it was Leon calling. Clearing her throat first, she pressed the green phone symbol to answer his call.

"Hello" said Sam in a low romantic voice.

"Hey, Baby. It's good to hear your voice."

"Really? And what does that mean for me?"

"It means that I enjoyed our romantic dinner on your birthday so much, that I was calling to ask you out again."

"You just want to get in my panties."

"That's not necessarily true. But to be honest, I have been missing that thing you do so well."

"Why don't you come by the house and let me fix you some spaghetti and garlic toast with a salad. And then we can play house. That way you can eat this cherry pie for dessert."

"What time should I be there?" Leon offered eager to get him some.

"I say around eight-thirty will be enough time for me to get everything finished and smelling just the way you like it."

"I'll see you then."

After Leon ended the call, he sat in his office reminiscing on some of the sexual escapades he and Sam had experienced. He recalled one particular trip to the casino when Sam had gotten tipsy from the shots of Cognac and the freak in her arose. She treated him to a forty-five minute blow job that ended in him discharging in her mouth. A cold chill came over his body at the thought of being served from head to toe.

Leon wrapped up the case file he was dealing with and cut the light off to leave. On his way home, he stopped by the florist and ordered a dozen long stem roses. He, showered, threw some jeans and a shirt on, and made a few calls before leaving the house.

He arrived at Sam's house a few minutes before eight-thirty. Leon fumbled through his glove compartment until he found the bottle of Joop. He sprayed himself a couple of times and put the cologne back in its spot. Leon approached the door and rang the bell, and within seconds, he could hear Sam unlocking the door. She opened the door in a Victoria's Secret negligee, ass out.

"Hey, Babe." Sam greeted him. She turned to walk off and Leon stared at her ass in a daze. He appreciated the way her ass clapped together when she walked, a talent above most women.

"Damn, Baby! You just answer the door without knowing who's behind it?"

"Naw, I just wasn't expecting anyone else at this time."

"It could've been anyone. It could have been the mailman with a package, it could've been" . . . Leon responded as he walked in and handed her the large vase.

"It could be this fine ass lawyer I know of, staring a hole through my back from watching this donkey as it wobble wobble."

Leon smiled, letting Sam know he approved her message. Although he was hungry, he couldn't wait for dessert, but Sam had fixed their plates and sat at the table across from him.

"This spaghetti is delicious." Leon said.

"I thank you kindly, Sir. It's my specialty." Sam replied and smiled.

Leon finished the first plate and went to the pot himself for a second serving. "Damn this food so good, it's like it's calling me."

"It is. You just don't know it yet."

Leon looked at Sam with a grin on his face as she picked the plates up and beckoned for him to join her. He quickly became erect as he started up the hallway, trailing closely behind her with his eyes zeroed in on the jiggle.

They made it to the bedroom and Sam wasted no time in introducing him to one of her many pleasures. She lay across the bed with her head hung off the edge, mouth opened wide.

"Come here, Baby, and put that thing in my mouth."

Leon moved to the edge of the bed and unsnapped his jeans. He reached in his boxers, pulled his dick out, and put it in her mouth. Sam slid the peppermint in her mouth and went to town on the dick. She sucked and gulped around his balls, completely saturating them with wetness. When she was finished, Sam blew on his nuts with her minty breath, causing Leon to shake with pleasure. When Sam felt the sudden jerk of his body, she knew he was about to cum.

"No, no! You gon' hold that in, Big Daddy." Sam said softly. She sat up in the bed and twisted her body around to face her lover.

"Now come get some of this pie for your dessert," Sam said as she leaned back and spread her legs wide.

Leon dropped the jeans to his knees and stepped out of them. He kneeled to the floor and pulled her body closer to the edge of the bed. He licked around the inside of her thighs, at times teasing her with his finger sliding in and out of her pussy. He nibbled on her pearl tongue and Sam laid back in ecstasy. She moaned and grunted as if she was already getting long-stroked. Leon lifted her hips off the bed and ran his tongue down the crack her of ass. Her eyes rolled to the back of her head. They cuddled together and were fast asleep. When Sam got up to make breakfast, Leon showered and shaved in her bathroom. When she came back to ask if he wanted one egg or two, he responded, "I just want you."

Sam smiled, thinking he was suggesting they hit it again, but instead, he pulled her into his arms and whispered, "Damn, girl! I missed you so bad."

"I missed you, too, a little bit,' Sam confessed without telling the whole truth.

"Well, let's do something about that."

"Something like what?" Sam asked.

Before she knew it, Leon reached into his pocket, took out a velvet box, went down on one knee, looked her in the eye and asked, "Samantha Williams, will you marry me?"

Sam was caught completely off guard. She never expected a proposal from Leon.

Her heart was fluttering and for once, she was at a loss for words. At this point in her life, she didn't think she'd ever marry. But the prospect sounded pretty good right then.

"Well?" he leaned in to her face.

She didn't even have to think about it. "Yes!" she blurted out!

He tipped up her chin and brought her lips to his, and they sealed the deal, so to speak, with a long, lingering kiss. She couldn't wait to tell Ingrid and Jonetta.

The Boss Take Over

Chapter 18

Graduation night came and just as she promised, Crystal's mentor, Miss Burnette, was front and center. Big Mama sat on the next row. A woman hidden under a black scarf and dark glasses sat next to her.

Crystal was excited to be graduating with her original class. Despite the fancy school that Jonetta enrolled her in, she had learned the meaning of the phrase, "there's no place like home." Her old home did not offer the lavish lifestyle the Barnes had provided, but it offered sanity to all things that she cherished. She embraced many of her childhood friends and picked up her school activities right where she left off before going to the West Coast. California was now a distant memory, eased by counseling and devoting her time to mentoring other youth. Miss Burnette had been pivotal in her healing, so Crystal was really happy to see her at graduation.

When the name "Crystal James" was called, the vibrant young teen strolled confidently across the stage. As she turned to see the pride on Big Mama's face, she caught a glimpse of the covered woman and wondered who she was. She made it back to her seat and looking around to see who was watching her, she focused on the woman in disguise. Her build resembled her Aunt Paulette, whom she hadn't seen since the day after they killed Boss. But it couldn't have been her, because Crystal knew she was dead. Not only did she know she was dead, but she knew exactly who had done it.

The last of the students' names were called and the graduating class was told to switch over their tassels. They proceeded out of the auditorium and Crystal anxiously waited to show her mentor some love for keeping her word. After giving her a big hug, she stepped back and they stood face to face.

"I'm so thankful to you for never giving up on me, Miss. Burnette, especially after the way I acted at first. I know I was a piece of work! Whew! Being the wild child that I was, I didn't think I had to answer any of your questions, but deep inside, I knew you were just trying to help me. Then when you checked me and made me face my past, I knew you were genuinely concerned about my well-being. For so long, I had hidden my issues and lashed out to conceal the pain eating at my soul. And then when I found out I was HIV positive, I really did want to kill myself. You saved my life."

"Crystal, I've always seen the greatest potential in you, even when your vision was too cloudy to see it for yourself. I knew you had the determination and the drive to excel beyond measures. That's why I decided to take you on as my special project. I was determined to get you back on the path of righteousness, but I wanted it to be done in a loving way. I really love you as a friend, Crystal, and I see us taking our friendship to new heights.

"One thing I always want you to remember, though," Miss Burnette continued, is when you're looking for the love of your life, take a look at yourself in the mirror. Make sure he sees the same beauty that you do. Make sure you find your king, not a nigga just looking some ass, for one night."

"Uh, excuse me? Aren't you being a little unprofessional right now?"

"I'm off government time today. This is friend time, so allow me to say what I mean and mean what I say," she said laughing.

"There's that hood background looming over the top of that college degree." Crystal replied with a smile.

"No, you didn't, OG Swirl."

The two burst into laughter and then embraced warmly. Crystal promised to continue her education and her work with the organization. She said goodbye to her mentor and turned to locate Big Mama, who was probably running her mouth with old friends. Scanning the crowd, she spotted the mysterious woman swiftly moving towards the exit. She rushed over to catch a glimpse of the woman and ran into a familiar face. Crystal stared at the elderly woman coming in her direction, but she couldn't place her. When Miss Jenkins sidled up to her and grabbed her right arm, the nervous teen froze in disbelief.

"Just be cool and don't make any sudden moves. Sudden moves require sudden action on my behalf. I'm here for your Aunt Paulette."

"But I haven't seen her in years." Crystal replied.

"She was just here."

"Where is she? I haven't seen her," Crystal said, realizing now that she may have been right about the mystery woman."

"The woman you were staring at when you walked across the stage a few minutes ago. She was dressed in all black, with a scarf across the top of her head sitting next to your grandmother."

Crystal was amazed that the elderly woman had scoped her every move. She pleaded for her safety and assured the older woman that she had nothing to do with Paulette or her ways.

"Listen here, Crystal. You tell Paulette she killed the last person on earth that I loved and she's going to have to answer, to me. Let her know she may as well stop running because we will meet sooner or later and

I always follow through with my word."

"I told you. I have nothing to do with Paulette. Who is it she supposedly killed?"

"My son, Trevon Barnes."

Crystal was shocked. She couldn't believe Trevon had been killed. She dropped her head and closed her eyes to see if somehow she could muster up the tears to pretend she cared, but she had long since finished crying over Trevon.

"I'm sorry to hear that Trevon is dead, but honestly I don't know anything about it. I left his house a long time ago."

"You tell Paulette what I said the moment you lay eyes on her. If you know what's good for you, you'll stay as far away as possible." Miss Jenkins said as she walked toward a waiting black Cadillac.

Now Crystal was really confused. All this time she thought either Trevon or Carson had killed her aunt back in California, especially since nobody in the family had heard from her. But even though she was family, Crystal blamed her for that episode with Boss. So if Paulette didn't care about her then, Crystal certainly didn't care about her now. She'd have to ask Big Mama about that.

Big Mama appeared at that moment, eyes red from crying at

the graduation. Crystal was the first of all her children and grandchildren to graduate from high school. After Crystal hugged her and then went off to party with her friends, Big Mama spent the rest of the day praising God, giving thanks, and cooking for the family celebration the next day.

A couple of days later, Crystal arrived home from a long day working with Miss Burnette on the big youth event that was coming up. She called out for Big Mama as usual, "but she didn't get a response. She had a sickening feeling in the pit of her stomach that something was wrong. When she didn't see her in bed or the bathroom, Crystal started to panic. Like so many older women in the projects, Big Mama was diabetic. She was finding it hard to walk these days, and the doctor had told her to stay off her swollen feet. But Big Mama was gonna do what Big Mama wanted to do, and nobody was going to tell her otherwise. Just as she was about to check with her closest neighbors, Crystal spotted a note on her dresser.

Dear Crystal,
I'll be at church late tonight to give God some praise. We're Having a revival. I was picked up by Sister Smith, Deacon Smith's wife, and she'll drop me off around 9:30 or so. I hope I didn't worry you. Come join us if you're not too tired.

Crystal exhaled, went to her room, and flopped across the bed to rest her exhausted brain. She drifted off for a moment until she was startled by a knock at her bedroom window. She pulled the curtain back and was surprised to see her Aunt Paulette squatting below the window in all black. Nervously, she opened the window and invited her in. She thought about the conversation with the older lady after graduation.

"Hey, Crystal."

"Hey, Aunt Paulette. What are you doing at the window? Why didn't you just come to the front like everybody else? Come on in. Big Mama's at church."

"No, I can't, Crystal. I haven't been around because I don't want to bring any heat to the family."

"Are you okay? I haven't seen you in a while. I thought you

were still in California."

"You can bet that I was at your graduation and I see you walk across that stage." Paulette replied proudly.

"I thought that was you sitting next to Big Mama in the black scarf and dark glasses."

"That wasn't me. I paid a home girl of mine to sit in like she was hiding from something so I could see if the old lady was following me for sure. I sat high in the seats watching her when she thought she was watching me. I saw her grab your arm at the end of the graduation ceremony when you thought you were chasing me. I wanted to walk up and snap her old ass neck, but I didn't want to expose my hand in front of so many witnesses."

"So, is Trevon really dead like she said he was?"

"He's dead as a door knob with no one to turn the handle. I'm waiting on the man right now to call me and let me know how much it's going to cost me to pour cement over his body. I wanted to make sure if his ass is reincarnated, he can never hurt you again."

"How did you know about that?"

"I have my ways."

"Well, I'm over all that. I've gone to counseling, and a beautiful lady, by the name of Pamela Burnette help me get myself together. I've learned to embrace the hand I was dealt and move on with my life. I'll be starting college in the fall.

"I've always wanted the best for you Crystal. I wanted you to do much better than any of us ever did." Crystal stared at Paulette as she remembered her meeting her at the L.A. airport, only to turn her over to Boss.

"Then why did you send for me to come to California to work for Boss? I'm talking about a man cold-hearted enough to kill his own mother!"

"I didn't know any better, Crystal. I was trying so hard to earn a man's love. I didn't think anything else was important. It's a revolving cycle, Crystal. Don't get caught up in it like I did."

"I won't, you can bet on that!" Crystal replied.

"How did you find out the maid was actually Boss's mother?"

Paulette asked, surprised, that Crystal knew the details of Miss Annie's demise.

Crystal took a deep breath and looked around outside. She spotted a slow moving Cadillac, but it quickly disappeared and she didn't think anything of it.

"After he beat me up," Crystal continued, "he tied a dog collar around my neck and took me to the basement. Before I hit the bottom step, the stench of decayed flesh filled the air and I nearly passed out. I was scared to death he'd do the same thing to me. I still have nightmares about that meat grinder in my sleep."

The young woman took a moment to regroup and then began again.

"So I played my position and did everything I could to keep him from getting angry. One night I told him he didn't have to beat me anymore. I was going to obey all of his rules, because I believed in him. That's when he let me out of the basement. From that point on, I felt like he had a heart of some kind, and he had to love his own mother. He came unglued and started to scream about why she had to go and what had happened to her. He even said you were the one that dragged her body to the basement."

Crystal looked directly into her aunt's eyes to get a reaction, but there was none. It was like she was staring at a pearl marble. She could see straight through to her aunt's battered soul.

She started again. "He ended up beating me for hours afterwards, saying that I knew too much and that I had to pay for it with my body.

"I'm so sorry for getting you caught up in all that." Paulette said woefully.

"Aunt Paulette, I'm your dead sister's only child! You should've been making sure I knew how to survive, not selling me out to the highest bidder!

"To be honest with you, I didn't know how to raise myself, let alone somebody else's child!"

"That's no excuse! Just know that I have forgiven you and I'm stronger for it."

A tear rolled down each side of Paulette's face like a moving snake. She looked into her niece's eyes and realized that Crystal had become the woman she'd never had the courage to be. She was beautiful, intelligent, vibrant, and most of all, forgiving. Paulette turned to walk away and Crystal called her back.

She reached through the window and grabbed her aunt tightly around the neck. Then she leaned over and whispered in her ear, Aunt Paulette, the next time you're looking for the love of your life, please do me a favor and take a long look at yourself in the mirror, and remember that you are beautiful enough to love yourself first."

Paulette was thankful for the inspirational words that came from her sister's daughter. She looked at her for a moment, and felt that she was looking at her sister again. She hugged her once more and when she turned to walk away, a slow moving car crept towards them with the lights off.

"Aunt Paulette!" Crystal screamed as the driver headed in her aunt's direction. But it was too late. The time had come for Boss's" bottom bitch" to meet the wrath of a scorned original to the game. Everything moved in slow motion as Miss Jenkins rolled down the window from the back seat.

A 380 with a silencer peeked out from the window of the driver's side, and a short "Puff" sounded in the air. Paulette fell in front of the window, covered by Crystal's screams. She was dead when she hit the ground. The Cadillac pulled off in the cover of darkness as Deacon and Sister Smith pulled up with Big Mama at the front door.

"No! Lord, no! Not again!" Big Mama screamed when she saw Paulette bleeding from the head. Crystal wrapped her arms around her as they both fell to their knees, crying in each other's' arms. Here she was again, mourning the loss of another daughter. Just how much could Big Mama bear?

Although she made it to the funeral, it was weeks before Big Mama would get out of bed. Crystal did all she could to take care of her, but it was as if Big Mama didn't really want to live anymore. She had lost two daughters, not to mention a granddaughter for a period of time. Crystal couldn't help but feel guilty, wondering if she could have saved her aunt by warning her about Miss Jenkins. She just didn't know.

All she could do was help Big Mama recuperate and manage her diabetes. Her feet were swollen again, this time so badly that it pained her to walk. Crystal had been taking care of her for several weeks now. One morning, when Crystal brought in Big Mama's breakfast, she called her over to the bed. Crystal eased up to the bed with an eerie feeling. She knew her Big Mama was sick, but she wasn't prepared for her to die.

"Crystal," Big Mama began," I'm getting pretty old now and I don't know if I'm going to get better this time. There are a few things I wanted to talk to you about."

"Yes, Big Mama. I'm listening," Crystal said nervously.

"First of all, I wanted you to know that I didn't abandon you when you came back from California. I knew you got hurt out there and Trevon and Jonetta thought they could take better care of you. They thought it would be good to get you out of the projects and it made sense to me at the time. It was never that I didn't want you. Your mother's been gone since you were a baby, and I knew I was getting too old to be the kind of mother you needed. That's why I let them take you. I just wanted you to know that."

Crystal breathed a sigh of relief. She was glad big mama didn't know the details of her California trip, but she'd always wondered why she gave her up.

"Second, I just wanted to let you know that you've been a beacon to this family. Despite everything that's happened to you, you're the only one to graduate and you helped the family, including me, whenever you could. I just wanted you to know that I love you, Crystal. I always have."

"Yes, Ma'am," Crystal smiled, patting her wrinkled hand.

"Finally, "I need you to promise me you will become the woman that no one in this family has ever been. I believe that you have the what it takes to make that happen, but you've got to get out of your own way and use that talent God gave you have to inspire other young women."

Tears were welling up in both their eyes.

Suddenly, the elderly woman started coughing and gasping for air.

"Big Mama, you alright?" Crystal asked as she moved closer.

"I'm fine for now, Baby, but the Lord has only kept me around to make sure that you understand what He wants you to do with your life."

"Big Mama, I love you so much!"

"I love you, too, Crystal, and if the Lord calls me home soon, remember what I told you."

Crystal kissed her grandmother on the forehead and returned to the kitchen.

"Big Mama, you want anything else while I'm in the kitchen?"

There was no answer. Crystal finished the dishes and returned to the room to find her Big Mama lying motionless with her eyes closed. She rushed over to feel for a pulse and was relieved when her eyes opened.

"Big Mama, you scared me. Didn't you hear me calling you a few minutes ago? I was asking you if you wanted me to bring you anything else from the kitchen."

"Unless you're gonna bring me some more salt for these eggs and more sugar for this coffee," she began.

"Now, you know I can't do that!" The doctor would kill me!" Crystal said, remembering the special diet rules the doctor had ordered.

"I know. I was just resting my eyes, preparing for a golden life on the other side, Crystal."

"Please don't talk like that, Big Mama."

"Crystal, we are on borrowed time in our lives. Anything over seventy becomes God's Fantastic Grace."

"But, I need you here to see me through the future!"

"No matter where I am, I'll be proud of whatever you do."

Crystal handed her grandmother the cup of coffee and walked away to cover her tears. Her crying was interrupted by a phone call.

"Hello," she answered.

"Good morning, Crystal. How are you?"

"I'm okay. Just a little worried about my grandmother."

"Is she going to be all right?

"I don't even know. I'm just going through the motions right now."

"Just have faith. In the meantime, I have some exciting news."

"What's going on?"

"You know that speaking tour that I told you about? It's all set up.

"That sounds great! When do I start?"

"I'm working on calling the schools to get permission to come in. It'll probably take less a few weeks. I should have an itinerary of dates and times real soon. You just start getting ready."

"It's good as done. This will take my mind off everything that's happened lately."

"You just hold your head up, Crystal, and I know that you'll become the star that I know you can be."

"Thanks so much, Miss Burnette. I needed that today."

"So do those kids. That's why it's inevitable we get started right away."

"That's the plan and I look to hearing from you."

Crystal felt rejuvenated and ready to face the world head-on with her story. Exhausted from all the thoughts that filled her head, she dozed off into a deep sleep.

The next morning, she headed to the kitchen to get her grandmother's breakfast. She put on the coffee and dropped a slice of bread into the toaster. She decided to ask Big Mama if she wanted anything in particular. So she opened her bedroom door.

"Big Mama, is everything alright this morning?" Crystal asked, but there was no response. She walked to the edge of the bed and called out to her again. There was still no answer. She checked her wrist for a pulse, but when she picked her grandmother's arm up, it was limp and cold. Apparently, she had been dead for hours. Crystal slumped over her body with deep sadness. For the second time in less than a month, she would have to plan a funeral.

Chapter 19

Trevon had been dead for six months. It was hard to believe that Jonetta's life had changed so much since then. The memories of the house and the terrible things that went on there were too much for her, and when Jonetta got of the hospital, she just didn't feel safe there anymore. She saw Trevon lurking around every corner in every room. Even before that horrible night, she couldn't bring herself to set foot in the media room. That had been Trevon's inner sanctuary, and there were too many reminders of the perverted sexual behavior that had controlled the last two years of his life, the things she had allowed to happen to Crystal. So she sold the house and got an apartment with Ingrid, who was now divorced.

The fact that Ingrid was an experienced nurse was a definite plus in accepting her offer to be roomies. Jonetta had lost a lot of weight that last year, and she just had no energy to do anything. Her appetite was poor and Ingrid was determined to monitor both her weight and her medicine toward full recovery. Sam came by two or three nights a week for movies and girl talk, so in many respects, it was just like old times: three sisters from the Como Projects just living out their lives.

Since Sam got back with Leon, she had become a different person: less angry, more loving, and more willing to be a really good friend to both of them. Before, her agenda had been more about what was in it for her, but once she finally settled into a serious relationship, she became more thoughtful and more generous to everyone she cared about. Unlike many women, she made sure her impending marriage would not put a damper on the quality and quantity of her time with her girls. The three of them were pretty much inseparable.

Sam would be meeting Ingrid and Jonetta at the Gaylord Texan this evening for a charity event. Leon's firm had bought a table for the event, and he had to be in court in Austin for a few days, so he gave the tickets to Sam to use with her friends. There would be good food, entertainment, and some really good speakers. Sam hoped the presenters on women's empowerment would motivate Jonetta to move on with her life.

God knows, she was trying, but she still had bouts of depression and she was as skinny as a rail. Before Trevon's death, she had given up hope and stopped taking her meds. She somehow thought dealing with AIDS would atone for not speaking up about Crystal's sexual abuse, for allowing it to go on. Whether it was her fear or her love of Trevon, she had allowed Crystal's life to turn down the same dark path that she had travelled, sexual abuse from a family member. When she lost her, she was devastated, and her break with Trevon just compounded the problem. But once she got back on her meds, her numbers improved and she started to feel better. Ingrid made sure that she stayed on track.

Her cell phone rang just as she glanced at the clock. It was Ingrid, calling from work to make sure she'd be ready when she got home. Ingrid could get ready for anything in twenty-five minutes or less, but Jonetta moved slowly and putting together an outfit was not as easy as it used to be.

Ingrid hung up the phone and slowly moved toward her closet to look for something that would fit the occasion. She grabbed a pair of her once tight-fitting slacks off the hanger and slid her thin frame inside, only to find out the pants were now three sizes too big. She looked down at her waist and tears spilled from her eyes when she saw how much weight she had lost.

She backed up, holding the loose pants up with her right hand, as she forced herself to look into the mirror. Like a figure in a horror movie, her rib cage was showing and her breasts had shriveled together like prunes. The once-glamorous half-breed hustler from the projects with the drop dead looks and tight body had dwindled to just above crack-head status. She shook her head in total disbelief of what she had depleted to as her eyes barely recognized her own image. Her hair was thinning and her once-vibrant skin was pale. She knew it was just a matter of time before death would relieve her and she had come to terms with it. She had prepared a will and written a long letter to each of her best friends, Ingrid, Sam, and Carson.

Jonetta overlapped the pants at the waist and tightened the belt to its last hole. She topped her ensemble with a loose-fitting long-sleeved tunic to mask her skeleton-like body, and then added an artsy scarf Sam had given her to detract attention from her emaciated frame. Her thinning hair fell limply about her shoulders so she pulled it back into a bun and surrounded it with a colorful headband. She might not look her best these days, but Sam had taught her how to be resourceful and put on a good front. She was as ready as she'd ever be to step out and have a good time.

Ingrid was on time, as always, and they arrived at the hotel fifteen minutes early, despite the heavy traffic on I-635. The two were seated at their table just off center stage. Sam, of course, would be fashionably late. She still liked to make an entrance by demanding the attention of every man in the room. Joining them at their table were two other attorneys, a paralegal, and a secretary from Leon's office.

Jonetta noticed that many of the tables were filled with youth groups, girls ranging from seven years of age all the way up to twenty-five, along with their sponsors and social workers. Most of them were girl scouts in uniform from all around the country. They seemed excited to be at such a fancy event. She scanned the room for any sign of Sam, but she was late, as usual.

The program began, with the Director of the Girl Scout of America, taking the podium to speak. She introduced herself and acknowledged a few of her colleagues and board members in the crowd.

"I'd like to thank everyone for joining us today. It's Girl's Scout Leader Appreciation Day! Whoo whoo! Give yourself a round of applause!" The enthusiasm was like a wave from table to table.

"Today we have some magnificent special guest speakers to give you young ladies something to take along with you in life. First off, I'd like to call out the Girl Scout leaders from every state to come up and join me right now on stage so that we all can acknowledge your presence." One representative from every state stood in front of the podium and the crowd gave them a standing ovation. The leaders ranged from eighteen to fifty, all dedicated, hard-working women who cared about the well-being of girls.

"These are the committed ladies that have become proven leaders in their communities. This group is the cream of the crop and they are prime examples of what we as administration would like all of you to become. Set your goals high like these role models have done and pursue of your destiny, day after day, until it becomes your truth."

The crowd went wild cheering on the director of programs.

"I'd like to introduce this next young lady and a former Girl Scout leader herself at one time. Please welcome to the wonderful and lovely Mrs. Pamela Burnette."

Miss Burnette advanced to the podium. "Hello friends and loved ones. I am thankful to God for being here today and happy to be in the presence of so many outstanding young ladies. To my younger up and coming generation, I see each and every one of you stars out there this evening. I want you to know that I recognize your talent and to the leaders of your state, I give you much respect, because I know the challenges one can face. I once was regional director of the North Texas Girl Scouts and I have an exciting young lady, a real fireball, with me today. She has a story worth of listening to. So without further ado, let's give a warm welcome to my good friend, Miss Crystal James." The crowd applauded.

Crystal eased up to the microphone and gazed out at the hundreds of onlookers in the building. She bowed her head for a moment for a final prayer that she touches someone's life with her words. When her head rose, she began to speak with authority.

"I'd like to thank Mrs. Jacque' Jones for allowing me the opportunity to speak to what I view as the young women of the future. I see the vibrant smiles on your faces out there today, and it gives me great joy to be in your presence."

Exhausted, Jonetta was doing all she could to stay awake. She didn't recognize the name "Crystal James" at first. But when the young woman at the podium began to speak, she recognized her voice immediately. Her hairstyle and makeup were different now, but there was no doubt about it. That was her Crystal. She was older, and obviously more mature. Jonetta could tell right away that her life had made a turn for the better.

She tapped Ingrid on the arm to see if she had noticed the speaker, but she was all ears to the gift of empowerment being delivered by the young woman.

"Unfortunately," Crystal continued, "I never had the opportunity of getting to know my mother from what was later written off as a car accident, shortly after I was born. With no other options for the future, I was raised in the housing projects where my grandparents had lived for years. My Big Mama (that's my grandmother for those of you who may not be familiar with that term), provided me with the tools to defend myself. She nurtured me with life and love, and taught me to be a lady at all times, even when no one was watching. I started out on a great path with much determination. I was a vibrant young girl, ready and willing to take life on with full force. I was excelling in everything I did, from academics to athletics. I was on the honor roll and I played basketball and volleyball. But the projects had its down side, too. There were gangs and drugs all around me. Some of my family members were not as loving as my Big Mama, and they tried to exploit my innocence.

"Then at sixteen, that life I so wished for and the innocence of my youth were snatched away from me. With the best of intentions, my Big Mama sent me on a vacation to visit one of her daughters on the west coast. She had been asking me to come out there, and I'd never even been out of Texas, so I saw this as an opportunity to see more of the world. I wanted to see movie stars and Disneyland. I thought this would be the best vacation I'd ever had. But I was wrong.

Knots were developing in the pit of Jonetta's stomach. She was suddenly afraid that Crystal would tell her whole story and reveal her part in it. She looked at Ingrid again to see if she recognized her, and saw tears streaming down her face. She knew.

"On that day," Crystal continued, "my whole life took a turn for the worst. I was forced to develop a sense of survival when I was delivered to a man that killed his own mother. He hated women, and he couldn't care less about any woman that he chose to manipulate and abuse. I was beaten and raped from the time I arrived until the day I was rescued, standing naked in the middle of the room with whelps covering my body. The people who rescued me seemed to have my best interests at heart, but later on, they started to abuse me, too. I wasn't beaten any more, but I was sexually abused by the man who saved me, and his wife just let it happen. I lived in a nightmare for the next two years.

With those words, Jonetta was afraid to look up again, fearful that the entire audience would know Crystal was talking about her. Ingrid reached around and hugged her shoulders, letting her know that she could get through this.

"I eventually became a runaway, and with the help of Miss Burnette, I was able to find my way back home to my Big Mama. Miss Burnette was my rock in helping me to survive my history of abuse. I wanted to die when I found out that I was HIV positive, but she helped me get through that as well. She convinced me that the disease was not a death sentence, and that I could lead a positive life by sharing my experience with others. I went back to Big Mama just a couple of months before she died, and I graduated from high school just in time for her to see that."

Jonetta's head was bowed, and the tears were flowing freely, but she could tell from the sounds of the room that she was not alone. There were people sniffling with tears streaming down their faces at almost every table. Ingrid passed her some tissues and hugged her again.

Crystal paused for a moment and took in a deep gasp of air to fight back the tears and get control of her emotions. She had not intended to revisit the atrocities of her past like this.

"By the grace of God I am standing before you today using the trials and tribulations of my past as the stepping stone to the words of wisdom I leave with you this evening. I was angry at everyone I knew for a while, and I blamed everything that happened to me on other people. But I brought a lot of my misfortune on myself. I acted out at school. I could have found a way to get help, but I didn't. Not for a long time. But I'm so glad that I had a chance to go back to my roots, to my Big Mama. She was a church-going woman, and she taught me about the power of forgiveness. She taught me that I needed to forgive the people that mistreated me for myself, not for them, because if I didn't, they would continue to steal my joy. I'd be consumed with my negative feelings about them. And I'm here to say that if I met any of them today, I would put my arms around them and hug them. I know I'm a better woman now.

Jonetta was outdone. She realized that Crystal's message was directed at her. And Crystal had forgiven her for the unforgiveable. She looked over at Ingrid and tears were streaming down her face. Her Crystal was now HIV positive! She wouldn't wish her condition on anyone, but especially not Crystal. While she wasn't directly responsible for giving it to her, she was still consumed with guilt. If she had acted, maybe this wouldn't have happened. But in Crystal's story, she saw that she took responsibility for her part in her misfortune, and then she forgave herself. That's exactly what was holding Jonetta back, she couldn't forgive herself. But if Crystal could do it, then maybe she could forgive herself as well. Crystal stepped back to the microphone and the crowd sat in awe of the young woman's courage she exudes in her presentation.

"To each and every one of you beautiful young ladies in attendance today, I want you to challenge yourselves to stay in school, stay focused on the future, and work to achieve your goals with integrity. Always be honest and decent to people, regardless of how they treat you. Don't hold on to grudges. That only hinders you from making progress. Let go and let God handle the burdens of your heart, because even though we think we are, were not always strong enough. Don't let your stubbornness block your blessings.

 Remember, ladies, when you're looking for the love of your life, make sure to take a long look at yourself in the mirror and recognize that you are a true beauty. Don't settle for any man that does not appreciate that. Be strong. And move on! Now everybody on your feet! Say this with me, and fill in your name. 'I am Crystal James, and I am a beautiful, intelligent, strong woman!'"

The crowd stood and repeated, "I am (saying their own names), beautiful, intelligent, strong woman!"

"Thank you!" Crystal said softly into the microphone. She brought both hands to her lips and blew a kiss out to the crowd. To thunderous applause, she scanned the entire room.

The crowd remained on their feet clapping for at least five minutes. Many were still crying from the powerful impact of Crystal's speech. Ingrid stood with her arms stretched out and heart wide open, feeling the young woman's pain in her words from knowing her story.

"She was awesome. That's my baby girl!" Jonetta whimpered in a barely audible voice.

"Yes, she is. And even though you can't admit it, you had a positive impact on which she is today. You heard her. It's time you forgive yourself."

Crystal stood at the podium, gazing out into the crowd, full of pride for her accomplishments and elated by the success of her speech. She felt a sense of relief from releasing the burdens of her past. Miss Burnette was right. She had cleared the pathway for a more promising and productive future. She stepped away from the podium, took a bow and raises her head with a smile on her face, holding her emotions deep inside.

While surfing the crowd, her eyes paused on a woman with her arms extended out in her direction, and then the built-up tears were loosened like a running levy. Crystal rushed off the stage in tears, barreling her way to the table where Ingrid stood.

"Aunt Ingrid!" Crystal grabbed her around her shoulders and hugged her tightly.

"Thank you, God, for answering my prayer. We found her! We found her in time! Thank you, Lord!" Ingrid responded with enthusiasm.

Crystal released her, stepping back to look at Ingrid as she tried to decipher what she had just said.

"In time for what?" she started. But her attention was caught by the woman beside her. She looked over at the slender woman in the baggy tunic sitting next to Ingrid. Crystal noticed the glossy look in her eyes, the sunken jaws, and the thinning hair. As she peered closely, she realized it was Jonetta, much changed since she last saw her coming out of the jail.

"Oh, my God! Mom, is that you?" Crystal stood surprised at how much weight Jonetta had lost. She reached down to hug her mom and felt the frail bones covered by her clothes.

Shaking nervously, she pulled the dying woman to her feet. With her hands rested on Crystal's shoulders, Jonetta looked into her eyes and made a strained effort to speak.

"It's me, Crystal. I just want to tell you how proud I am of you.

Your speech was so moving. And I'm sorry for the pain that I caused by standing behind a man that I knew in my heart was abusing you. Please forgive me."

Crystal was careful to hug her adopted mother lightly. She'd felt the frailness of her body through her clothes the first time she hugged her.

"Mom, I forgive you. Weren't you listening to my speech? Now that I've gotten older, I understand how hard it is for a woman to turn against a man that she has come to love and depend on. I know you didn't want to believe what was going on. I hated you up until that point because I felt like you did nothing to stop what was happening to me, especially since you'd been abused as a child. But I realize now, that in many ways, you were a victim of Trevon's sickness as much as I was."

Jonetta sobbed as Crystal hugged her again.

Miss Burnette eased back to the podium to get the program back underway.

She tapped on the microphone. "Can I have everyone's attention please?"

The audience had started to talk amongst one eat other at their tables and were not moved at all by her plea to gain crowd control. Instead, those nearby continued to watch the three women with tears running down their faces as they took turns embracing each other. Recognizing Miss Burnette's attempt to resume the program, they moved out of their seats and headed toward the lobby. With Ingrid on one arm and Jonetta on the other, Crystal led them to the back of the large room.

As they approached the exit, they all saw her at the same time.

Sam yelled out, "Hey, ya'll! I see everybody made it!

"Where have you been?" demanded Ingrid.

"Sorry I was late. That traffic on 635 was a monster!"

Ingrid and Jonetta looked at each other and smiled, knowing that Sam was lying.

"Well, I'm here now. What I miss?"

"The best speech you ever heard in your life! Don't you see who this is?"

Sam's mouth dropped and her eyes widened as she recognized the third member of their party. "Crystal! How you been, Baby?"

"Hi, Aunt Sam," Crystal laughed as she hugged her. "You haven't changed a bit!"

"I know, girl. You can't improve on perfection." Sam quipped, repeating her most famous words. "So what's happening with you?"

"I am getting myself together and moving forward. I work with Miss Burnette and her non-profit group by mentoring and speaking to young women. I tell my story at events like this one."

"That's wonderful, Crystal! Are you going to school?"

"I just graduated from the Heights, my old school in the neighborhood. I'll be starting college in the fall."
Jonetta beamed at Crystal's latest announcement.

"Where are you going?" Ingrid interjected.

"I have a scholarship from the foundation to the University of Houston. I'll be leaving next month."

"That's wonderful! I'm so glad you were able to turn your life around!" Sam replied.

"And we are so proud of you!" Jonetta added.

Miss Burnette interrupted with her announcement that the raffle Would be taking place in a few minutes. First prize was a vacation to the Bahamas. This was the last chance to get tickets in the lobby.

"Ooh, girl! I got to go get me some tickets. You know how I love me a vacation. And I'm feeling lucky!"

As she waited for the ticket stubs, Miss Burnette came over to their table. "You gave a beautiful speech, Crystal! I'm so proud of you! I know you've made a difference in someone's life today."

"Thank you, Miss Burnette. Like you said, once I started, I wasn't nervous at all. I think I might major in communications at UH."

"That would be perfect for you. And I'm so glad the 'For the Beauty of a Woman' foundation could help you in your endeavors. You've worked so hard. You deserve it."

"Thank you," Crystal beamed with pride.
Sam returned with five tickets for each of them. They all took their seats again, as Sam nodded to the others at the table. Since she

stopped by her fiancé's office all the time, she knew them all.

"Well, hello, Samantha! I'm so glad you made it. I was afraid you'd missed Crystal's speech when I didn't see you."

Ingrid, Jonetta and Crystal all turned to Sam in shock. She knew Pamela Burnette! She had known all along that Crystal would be speaking, and she planned this event to reunite them.

"Actually, I heard it all from the back," Sam responded. I was running late and I didn't want to attract attention to myself once she started. Crystal, you were off the chain! I am so proud of you!"

Tears were streaming down Jonetta's face again. Sam reached over and squeezed her frail hand.

"Miss Burnette!" Crystal interrupted, trying to take the tension off the moment. "Do you know everyone here? Besides you and my Big Mama, these are the women that made me who I am today. I want to thank you all for that. I love you!"

"We're ready for the raffle now, Miss Burnette!" one of the volunteers called out.

"Excuse me," Miss Burnette said as she headed back to the stage.

Crystal watched her mentor travel back to the podium. She should have taken her place back on stage with the other speakers and officers, but she did not want to leave the circle of women who had served as her "mamas" during the most crucial period of her life. Without a doubt, she had missed them.

Ingrid leaned over to Sam. "How do you know Pamela Barnett, Sam? You don't exactly move in the same circles."

"You don't know who I know, Miss Thang."

Ingrid just shook her head at Sam's response.

"Okay, I'll tell you. I went by Leon's office one day to meet him for lunch, and she was there pitching this foundation and selling tickets to this banquet. She got to bragging about this young girl she was mentoring who would be speaking at the program. When she said her name was Crystal James, I just put two and two together and thought I'd hook everybody up. Mostly, I wanted to give Jonetta some peace. She's been worried sick about her since she ran away."

"Sam, you are too much!"

"We're family," Sam responded. "And there's nothing I wouldn't do for ya'll."

Miss Burnette began, "First, I'd like to thank you all for your support of our new foundation with both your contributions and your presence this evening. Please give yourselves a round of applause."

The clapping echoed throughout the room.

"Now," Miss Burnette continued," we'd like to show our thanks to you by giving a few gifts of our own. Some of these were made possible by our generous donors as well, and once again, we thank you."

After more applause, she continued, "So let's get on with this raffle!"

Sam, Ingrid, Jonetta, and Crystal divided up the tickets that Sam had plopped down on the table. Sam figured the odds were good that at least one of them would win something. She wanted the trip to the Bahamas for two. It would make a great honeymoon getaway.

"The first drawing is for a day of pampering at Spa, Baby! The number is 43217!"

The women scanned their tickets but neither of them had the number.

"We just did that anyway, Ingrid," Sam pouted.

An excited blond across the room yelled out," That's me! I won!"

"Come on down with your ticket and claim your prize at the first table!" Miss Burnette instructed.

"The next prize will be a weekend getaway for two at the Four Seasons in Dallas. This fabulous hotel features luxurious rooms with all the amenities and a breakfast buffet you will just love! The winning number is 34281!"

Again, the women examined their tickets. Ingrid thought she might win when the first three numbers were called, but the last two were twenty digits away.

"That would be me," a handsome looking man remarked as he stood holding his ticket in the air.

"Come on down to the first table, Sir," Miss Burnette directed.

"I wonder if he's married," Sam remarked.

"You oughta quit that! You're engaged!" Ingrid said.

"I may be engaged, but I ain't dead!" Sam answered.

The entire table laughed at Sam's flippant remark. Then, remembering who was seated at her table, she quipped, "Don't tell Leon I said that!"

"Our final raffle," Miss Burnette continued, for the paid vacation for two to the Bahamas goes to number 36794!"

There was a long pause as people carefully perused their ticket stubs. Sam examined all five of hers, and then started looking at those of her friends. Spotting the winning number on the table, she yelled out," You won! Jonetta, you won!"

Jonetta, still overcome from her reunion with Crystal, smiled feebly.

"Really? I won?"

"Yeah, girl! That's you! 36794!" Sam yelled out, "We got it! We got it!"

Miss Burnette smiled as she motioned Sam down to the front.

"I can't. . ." Jonetta mumbled shyly."

"Yes, you can, girl. Come on. We got you!"

Sam took one arm and Crystal took the other as they helped Jonetta slowly maneuver her way to the front. Ingrid followed right behind them with their purses.

"Thank you," Jonetta whispered on the way down. But you bought this ticket, Sam. You should go. You know I'm not up to it."

"Don't worry about that. We'll just wait till you're feeling better. You're gonna do this thing."

"I don't know, Sam. And I'd hate to pick just one person to go with me. You know I can't do it alone."

"You don't have to choose, Jonetta. I told you I got you! You take the tickets for you and Crystal. I'll pay for me and Ingrid. Problem solved. Now, what you got to say about that?"

The four of them moved slowly, like battered soldiers coming home from war. The entire audience could see how sick Jonetta was, and although they did not know why, they gave her a standing ovation.

"Not a damn thing, Sam. Not a damn thing." Jonetta said, tears streaming down her face.

The life and journey of a man destined to succeed

I AM AUTHOR J. W. SMITH WRITER,
INSPIRATIONALSPEAKER AND MOTIVATOR TO ALL. I
WAS BORN AND RAISED IN ONE OF THE TOUGHEST
NEIGHBORHOODS IN LOS ANGELES, CALIFORNIA. AT A
VERY YOUNG AGE, I WAS TAUGHT TO SURVIVE BY ANY
MEANS NECESSARY OR FALL VICTIM TO THE STATISTIC
OF SOCIETY IN THE EARLY 80'S WHEN THE CRACK
EPIDEMIC HIT, I LOST MY FATHER'S GUIDANCE AND
TEACHINGS TO THE DRUG COCAINE AND MY VIRGINITY
TO THE STREETS. WITH A LENGTHY SENTENCE AHEAD
OF ME AND ONLY A HIGH-SCHOOL DIPLOMA TO FALL
BACK ON, I DILIGENTLY SET OUT TO WRITE MY FIRST
NOVEL "NO LOVE LOST", WHILE THE SPIRIT OF GOD
PROVIDED THE FAITH AND THE STRENGTH TO
CONQUER THE OBSTACLES I WOULD SOON FACE IN
DOING SO. AFTER MANY YEARS OF INCARCERATION
BOTH AS A JUVENILE AND AN ADULT, I FINALLY WOKE
UP AND STARTED TAKEN RESPONSIBILITY FOR MY
OWN ACTIONS RATHER THAN CONTINUING TO SEARCH
FOR BLAME IN OTHERS. I AM THE PROUD FATHER OF
THREE YOUNG ADULT TWO GIRL AND MY 23 YEAR OLD
YOUNG MAN, WITH THE YOUNGEST GRADUATING HIGH
SCHOOL AND SET FOR TEXAS AM COLLEGE THIS
SEMESTER. THE FACT THAT I SEE MY OLDEST
DAUGHTER, WHO WAS IN A TRAGIC ACCIDENT AT THE
AGE OF 16, PARALYZED FROM THE WAIST DOWN AND
STILL EXUDE THE KIND OF DETERMINATION THAT SHE
DOES TO WALK AGAIN, GIVES ME THE MOTIVATION TO
FIGHT HARDER IN BECOMING A SUCCESSFUL
PROVIDER, ENTREPRENEUR AND ENCOURAGEMENT TO
ALL. THE PERSEVERANCE AND DEDICATION WITHIN
ALLOWS ME TO FIND GUIDANCE IN WHAT
BOOKLOVERS ANTICIPATE. I AM THE C.E.O OF
SHINNING STARR PUBLICATIONS WITH SEVERAL
AUTHORS' IN THE MAKING ON THE ROSTER. WHEN I'M
NOT WRITING I AM ENJOYING A DAY OF RELAXATION
WITH THE FAMILY OR CATCHING UP ON THE POLITICAL

WHOA'S OF THE WORLD. I AM AUTHOR J.W SMITH AND
LEAVING A LEGEND TO BE REMEMBERED BY IS WHAT I
AWAKE EVERY MORNING WITH THE ANTICIPATION OF
DOING.ABOUT THE AUTHOR

www.ingramcontent.com/pod-product-compliance
Lightning Source LLC
LaVergne TN
LVHW051626080426
835511LV00016B/2197